SIN.

GUILT.

FORGIVENESS.

SIN.

GUILT.

FORGIVENESS.

A Biblical Understanding of Christian Truths

SMITA VALENTINA

SIN.
GUILT.
FORGIVENESS.

A Biblical Understanding of Christian Truths

First printed edition 2024

Published by: **Notion Press Media Pvt. Ltd.**

[5]Let the wise listen and add to their learning,

and let the discerning get guidance –

Proverbs 1:5

To,

You

AN INTRODUCTION

The story of the conception of a book is as important as the book itself. It guides us in understanding the purpose of the book and enables us to peruse it to that end.

This small book on Sin-Guilt-Forgiveness offers a comprehensive biblical understanding of vital Christian truths that are foundational to a holy living as called by God. This book is for the Christian who is willing to introspect, learn and be equipped to bear much fruit for the glory of God.

The seed for this book was sown in my heart when I was invited to share the Word of God in a small fellowship in *Jorhat, Assam*. Soon it turned into a fairly regular opportunity and I was challenged. I have known the members of this beautiful community for quite a while and their dedication and zeal for the Lord Jesus Christ has always inspired me. As I began preparing my messages I was filled with a deep sense of unworthiness. *Who am I to be granted this blessing to stand in the House of God and encourage His saints! What was I to share with this congregation that is so firmly rooted in the Word of God! What was I to bring forth for them who already manifest the fruit of the Holy Spirit in their lives!*

God has not granted me this wonderful privilege because I deserve it; rather, as I gradually realized, God has given me this opportunity to draw nearer to Him. I would have never even thought of exploring the themes of Sin-Guilt-Forgiveness in such depth had it not been for the challenge to spur the saints of *JCF*. As I began pondering over the themes I could explore for this particular group of Christians, as led by the Holy Spirit, I knew that my messages ought to be introspective and challenging. They must be like reminders about truths we often forget or take for granted. They must be deeper revelations that would enable the congregation of believers to grow in full-maturity in the likeness of Jesus Christ.

One of the leaders of the Church had expressly told me: *I want our congregation to become spiritually mature. We want solid spiritual food.* Solid spiritual food can at times be difficult to digest but it is essential for spiritual maturity.

One of the greatest challenges in our Christian journey is overcoming our spiritual weaknesses. Often, they can be quite subtle and an un-armoured Christian can easily overlook the early signs of spiritual weakness in his or her own life as well as in the body of Christ. It is so challenging to diagnose because most of us are not sufficiently spiritually discerning to point it out to the others. At the same time, most of us are not spiritually mature to receive the diagnosis without resentment. To add to that, many a times we suffer from the vice of *selective hearing*. But being aware of our own spiritual status is vital to our faith and witness. If we are oblivious to our spiritual weaknesses we are at great risk of getting side-tracked and leading others astray.

The inspiration for this book began with my meditations on 'GUILT'. As prompted and enlightened by the Holy Spirit, it grew on to include a holistic understanding of God's Law, Sin and Forgiveness. The themes this book covers draws from the real struggles of Christians. In my interactions with many born-again Christians, I have found that we still struggle with the proper biblical understanding of Sin-Guilt-Forgiveness. The Devil is on the prowl and unfortunately, he has invaded our earthly churches. We often think that the

Devil targets naïve, spiritual infants. We can't be more wrong. I recall J.R.R. Tolkien's *Lord of the Rings*. The ring of power was ultimately destroyed by the hobbit, *Frodo Baggins*. When Frodo offered the ring to Gandalf, the mighty Wizard refused saying – *"Don't tempt me Frodo! I dare not take it. Not even to keep it safe. Understand Frodo, I would use this ring from a desire to do good. But through me, it would wield a power too great and terrible to imagine."* [Dialogue from *The Fellowship of the Ring*]

The Devil knows that if he manages to win over one church leader, he can win over the entire church. We see it happening all around us. Paul warned: *"Everything is permissible" – but not everything is beneficial. "Everything is permissible" – but not everything is constructive.* **(1 Corinthians 10:23).** Today, there are churches that are under the control of the Devil that just use the phrase *"Everything is permissible"* as a license for all forms of immorality. *Come just as you are to worship* is misinterpreted as coming drunk and drugged, coming is provocative clothing with no regard for the sanctity of God's House. The church has become indistinguishable from a nightclub with loud music and a sermon with random verses strung together that appease people and approve of their ways. For a herd of sheep, nothing can be more dangerous than a shepherd who himself does not know the way and is led by the Devil.

All wisdom and knowledge is already present within the Bible, yet it becomes an uphill task arranging all the invaluable information into meaningful answers to the questions we struggle with. I request you to read this book meditatively and try to examine yourself.

I owe every piece of insight contained within this book to the Holy Spirit who has worked in me and through me day and night and even in visions and dreams to bring forth this enlightenment. I am just a mere, unworthy instrument in the hand of God and I am humbled that God has chosen me and equipped me to encourage my fellow-believers that we can run our Christian race together in faith.

This book is built on the foundation of the Word of God and brought forth through the inspiration of the Holy Spirit. I also acknowledge that the Holy Spirit has guided me in using my own life experiences and my learnings from others around me to bring more clarity on the themes discussed in this book. These learnings have come from a wide range of sources – my family, friends and relatives, churches and fellowships I have been associated with even if for a brief period of time, colleagues, and even strangers. May our good God reward them all for their contributions! I also acknowledge that there are many who uphold me in their prayers. I may not know each one of them, but God knows each one of you by name and He is faithful in rewarding those who do good. Thank you for your prayers.

Now, I dedicate this book to all who will read it – present and future. What more can I say than this: *I believe, God predestined that this book should land in your hands. Please read it prayerfully and it is my prayer that it will help you in your spiritual growth.*

Dear Heavenly Father, I pray that You bless this book and use it for Your glory and for the strengthening of Your children here on this earth. In Jesus' name I pray, Amen.

I

GOD'S LAW & SIN

God's Law & Sin

Smita Valentina

I

Sin is lawlessness. Sin separates us from God. Honestly speaking, we all sin. Even after accepting the gift of Salvation and the power to say 'No' to sin; we often find ourselves struggling with sin. Jesus says – *"I tell you the truth, everyone who sins is a slave to sin."* **(John 8:34)**

Jesus Christ came into this world to take away the sins of the world. Then, why do we sin? If you ask any Christian, they will all agree that we should not sin. But most will struggle to explain 'what constitutes sin'. I have found that many Christians still dwell in highly abstract ideas about sin and law. No wonder, we struggle to fully comprehend the gift of Salvation.

Through the inspiration and guidance of the Holy Spirit, in this section, I have tried to condense a holistic idea of God's Law and Sin. We will try to understand, the uniqueness of God's Law and its eternal validity. We will look into the various components of the Mosaic Law and their applicability under the Old and the New Covenants. We will try to understand the ways in which we may continue to sin even after we are born-again. At the same time, we will look into Law and righteousness under the New Covenant.

It's my prayer that as you read this book, you will have a clearer understanding of 'sin' and you will find answers to many of your questions related to sin, salvation and holy living.

UNDERSTANDING GOD'S LAW

Let me begin with an illustration:

Every nation and every community has some laws. When monarchy was the predominant form of government the King or the Monarch set the laws that were to be obeyed by all the residents of his kingdom. Today, most independent nations have democratic and republican form of government. People's representatives, in case of India – the Parliament, set the laws of the land. Since people are fallible and imperfect, it is only natural that the laws set by them are also imperfect. Therefore, time and again we encounter opposition against laws that appear unfair or discriminatory.

In a monarchy it was not unusual to find kings being whimsical in setting laws. For instance, in the **Book of Esther** we read of King Xerxes. At the behest of a favoured royal official, Haman, King Xerxes let him issue an edict *to destroy, kill and annihilate all the Jews – young and old, women and little children – on a single day, the thirteenth day of the twelfth month, the month of Adar, and to plunder their goods. A copy of the text of the edict was to be issued as law in every province and made known to the people of every nationality so they would be ready for that day.* (Ref. **Esther 3:13-14**)

Can we call this law just and fair?

Democracies claim to be better than monarchies. However, evidence suggests most democracies are oligarchies with power concentrated in the hand of a few. The 'few' may be dominant communities or business corporations or wealthy individuals or even the mafia. The general charge against the laws set by such democracies is that the laws of the land favour the 'few' while it is exploitative to the general populace especially the poor and the minority communities. For instance, many Indian states have banned the sale and

Smita Valentina

consumption of certain meats. Some cities enforce strict vegetarianism thereby outlawing the sale and consumption of non-vegetarian food items within the city premises.

Can we call these laws just and fair?

It is not necessary that all laws, whether in monarchies or democracies or any other form of government, are unfair. There are certain universal standards that are accepted by almost all nations and nationalities. One such document is the Universal Declaration of Human Rights. One stark feature of all such laws and standards formulated by human beings is that they are dynamic. These laws are ever changing, ever shifting. For instance, till recently homosexuality was considered unlawful by almost all nations and nationalities despite its prevalence since ancient times. Today, same-sex marriages are legal in nearly 35 countries. Homosexuality is widely accepted in the more developed countries. Some countries tolerate it, while homosexuality is a punishable offence in the countries that follow Islamic law.

How do we navigate such legal complexities?

When a person breaks the laws of the land it is called a *crime*. **SIN**, on the other hand, involves breaking moral and religious laws. In the case of Christians, SIN is about breaking the Covenant Law or failing God's standards. All sins are not crimes and all crimes are not sins. In some cases, like the Islamic nations where their national laws are closely linked with their religious laws, the overlap between sin and crime is much greater than many secular countries where the overlap can be quite minimal.

When talking about SIN from the Christian standpoint, we need to visualize being residents of a Kingdom ruled by the King of kings i.e. the GOD in the Bible. This analogy of God being our King and we being His subjects is widespread in the Biblical text. In fact, before Israel got their first king as King Saul, the elders of Israel gathered together and demanded Samuel a 'king' to lead them. Samuel was displeased and he prayed to the LORD. And the LORD told him, *"Listen to all that the people are saying to you; it is not you they have rejected, but they have rejected me as their king."* (Ref. **1 Samuel 8:4-7**)

It is interesting that much before the events of Samuel, God had foretold through Moses that Israel would eventually reject the LORD as their King and like all the nations around them set a king over themselves. In fact, God had also provided the guidelines for the office of the king. (Ref. **Deuteronomy 17:14-20**)

So, when we are the citizens of the Kingdom of God, we are to keep the law that is set by God. **Philippians 3:20** tells us – *But our citizenship is in heaven.* In my meditation of the Word of God, I have found the following qualities of God's Law that surpass all the worldly laws:

Smita Valentina

Psalm 19:7-14 is an ode to God's perfect law –

⁷The law of the LORD is perfect, reviving the soul.
The statutes of the LORD are trustworthy, making wise the simple.
⁸The precepts of the LORD are right, giving joy to the heart.
The commands of the LORD are radiant, giving light to the eyes.
⁹The fear of the LORD is pure, enduring forever.
The ordinances of the LORD are sure and altogether righteous.
¹⁰They are more precious than gold, than much pure gold;
They are sweeter than honey, than honey from the comb
¹¹By keeping them is your servant warned; in keeping them there is
great reward.

¹²Who can discern his errors? Forgive my hidden faults.
¹³Keep your servant also from wilful sins; may they not rule over
me.
Then will I be blameless, innocent of great transgression.

¹⁴May the words of my mouth and the meditation of my heart be
pleasing in your sight,
O' Lord, my Rock and my Redeemer.

Psalm 19 provides us with quite a comprehensive list of the merits of God's Law.

1.   God's Law is perfect.

First and foremost, King David – the Psalmist, says that the law of the LORD is perfect.

In the present times, almost nothing is hidden from the media. We often witness people accused of certain wrongdoings question the law. Their attorneys try to twist the words of the law to prove that the wording of the law is confusing. They would argue that the law needs changing. Seldom would we come across an accused that would defend the law. But time and again in the Bible, we come across people who sinned grievously and yet accepted the perfection of the law of the LORD.

Apostle Paul writes to the Romans – *So then, the law is holy, and the commandment is holy, righteous and good.* (Ref. **Romans 7:12**)

2. God's Law is trustworthy, right and altogether righteous

I have so often been disappointed by the laws of the land. First of all, there are so many laws and frequently they clash against each other. It appears that they are designed to confuse the citizens to penalize them. The laws appear to have been designed not to help the citizens but to protect the government or those who influence the government. However, when I read God's laws throughout the Bible that spans thousands of years and multiple generations, I find they continue to hold firmly to the central principle – *Love the LORD your God and love one another.* No other law can be more trustworthy than God's law.

3. The Law of the LORD is delightful

I am sure that no one finds following laws very appealing. How often do we drive over the speed-limit or grudgingly give our taxes! Laws almost always appear exploitative and cumbersome. However, King David says that the Law gives joy to him. In **Psalm 119:174**, he says – *Your law is my delight.*

4. God's Law gives light and life.

The Book of Deuteronomy is a summary of all that happened through Exodus-Leviticus-Numbers. Moses was forbidden to cross the river Jordan and before handing over his leadership to Joshua, he recapitulated God's faithfulness and laws in his address to the nation of Israel. The following verses highlight the purpose of God's laws:

Smita Valentina

i. *Follow them so that you may live and may go in and take possession of the land that the LORD, the God of your fathers, is giving you.* (**Deut. 4:1**)

ii. *Observe them carefully, for this will show your wisdom and understanding to the nations, who will hear about all these decrees and say, "Surely this great nation is a wise and understanding people."* (**Deut. 4:6**)

iii. *Be careful to obey so that it may go well with you and that you may increase greatly in a land flowing with milk and honey, just as the LORD, the God f your fathers, promised you.* (**Deut. 6:3**)

iv. *Now choose life, so that you and your children may live and that you may love the LORD your God, listen to his voice, and hold fast to him. For the LORD is your life.* (**Deut. 30:19-20**)

Psalm 119:105 says – *Your word is a lamp to my feet and a light for my path.* God's laws show the way for holy living and the only way to know God more closely. Obeying God's laws brings blessings. They are aimed at bringing glory to God, fostering love and fellowship with God and with one another and bringing an abundant life.

5. The Law of the LORD is worth pursuing

Psalm 19 calls the Law of the LORD more precious than gold and sweeter than honey. The Law is so precious because of its life-saving and live-giving nature. Following the Law prevents us from committing wrongs that impact us as well as the people around us.

The Law warns us of the perils of forbidden acts and protects us from harming ourselves as well as others. The warning itself should discourage us from committing sins; however we frequently choose death over life because of the stubbornness of our heart.

Many argue about the usefulness of the Law. **Hebrews 7:18-19** says – *The former regulation is set aside because it was weak and useless for the law made nothing perfect…* Taken out of context, verses such as these can be misused by unscrupulous people to advocate that the God's Law is meaningless.

Let me put this into perspective: Can we call a lighthouse 'useless' because a ship ignored its beacon and collided against another incoming ship? Or, can we say a "Beware of Dog" sign is useless if a trespasser chooses to break into a house ignoring the sign and gets mauled by the guard dog? Just like the lighthouse or the "Beware of Dog" sign, the Law of the LORD is a beacon that shows us what is right and what is wrong. The Word of God also carries immense encouragement motivating us to choose the right. However, the onus of choice lies on us. If we choose to obey the Law, we choose life – we choose God to be our King and we choose the citizenship of the Kingdom of God. But when we choose death – we reject God as our King and forfeit our citizenship of the Kingdom of God.

6.   God's Law reveals God's nature

The Law of the LORD tells us about God's character. God revealed Himself to Moses in a limited way in **Exodus 34**. God Himself proclaimed that He is compassionate, gracious, slow to anger, abounding in love and faithfulness. God proclaimed himself to be forgiving as well as just.

As we meditate on God's Laws we understand His great sacrificial love for even the lowliest of sinners. We understand that God doesn't show favouritism. The more we know of God's Law, the more we are in awe of God's goodness and faithfulness. We get a glimpse of His holiness and glory and grow in reverential fear towards God.

Smita Valentina

7. God's Law reveals God's will

Just as the Law reveals God's nature, it also reveals God's will. People have a penchant for the theatrical. When Naaman came to Elisha to be healed of his leprosy, the prophet asked him to wash himself seven times in the Jordan. This enraged Naaman. He had expected some grand gesture. He was about to return unhealed when his servants reasoned that if the prophet had asked Naaman to do something great he would have done it, so why not do this simple thing of washing himself in the Jordan seven times. (Ref. **2 Kings 5:8-14**)

When we think of God's will, we always imagine something grand – big ministry, grand church, thousands upon thousands in attendance, a super-hit music track, mission work in the most difficult areas… I too fostered such grand ideas once upon a time, but the Word of the LORD admonished me – *What does the LORD your God ask of you but to fear the LORD your God, to walk in all his ways, to love him, to serve the LORD your God with all your heart and with all your soul, and to observed the LORD's commands and decrees that I am giving you today for your own good.* (Ref. **Deut. 10:12-13**)

Micah 6:8 also reiterates the same – *He has showed you, O man, what is good. And what does the LORD require of you? To act justly and to love mercy and to walk humbly with your God.*

THE VALIDITY OF OLD TESTAMENT LAW

However, when we read portions of the New Testament, the validity of the Law starts confusing us. **Romans 7:6** says – *But now, by dying to what once bound us, we have been released from the law so that we serve in the new way of the Spirit, and not in the old way of the written code.*

Romans 10:4 says – *Christ is the end of the law so that there may be righteousness for everyone who believes.*

Furthermore, **Galatians 3:23-25** says – *Before this faith came, we were held prisoners by the law, locked up until faith should be revealed. So the law was put in-charge to lead us to Christ that we might be justified by faith. Now that faith has come, we are no longer under the supervision of the law.*

This leads many to question: If Christ is the end of the law then does the law stands null and void now? What does it mean when the Bible says Jesus fulfilled the law? Are we no longer bound by the law? So if the law stands nullified, does it mean there is no sin? After all, if there are no laws to break, how does one sin?

[We must understand that we are not the original recipients of the Epistles. The Apostles addressed the believers of their time many of whom were Jews who had accepted Jesus Christ. Many of these converts were unable to let go of the ceremonial law because it was embedded in their cultural fabric. When these converts began preaching the gospel to non-Jews, they continued emphasising on existing Jewish traditions as well. For example – Many Jewish converts continued to emphasise on circumcision.]

Many have interpreted these verses to claim once we accept Christ Jesus as our personal Saviour and are born again, our sins don't matter to God. Some have even used it as a license to sin.

These are pertinent questions which only get more confusing when the Apostles challenge us – *What then? Shall we sin because we are not under law but under grace? By no means!* **(Romans 6:15).** *No one who lives in him (Christ Jesus) keeps on sinning. No one who continues to sin has either seen him or known him.* **(1 John 3:6)**

So, what exactly is the New Testament talking about when it speaks of SIN and LAW?

The Law given by God through Moses to Israel is often termed the Mosaic Law. This Mosaic Law consists of a body of various kinds of instructions and commands that span through the books of Exodus, Leviticus, Numbers and Deuteronomy. The entire body of Mosaic Law addresses a wide variety of topics like: the Ten Commandments, social responsibilities, laws of justice and mercy, various festivals and how to celebrate them, regulations for Sabbath, various kinds of offerings, instructions for hygiene, unlawful sexual relations, rules for priests, punishment and atonement for sins, etc.

These were essential rules of holy living for Israel. While in the wilderness, God dwelt with Israel as a cloud during the day and a pillar of fire at night. However, living amongst cultures that practiced idolatry, Israel wanted a physical symbol to direct their worship to. In the Book of Genesis we never see God demanding any special offering. When we read about offerings made by people, it was their voluntary act of worship perhaps influenced by the prevalent cultures. When Israel expressed her desire to worship God in visible ceremonial ways like the other cultures around her, God laid down specific guidelines to set Israel apart from the other nations around her.

The Mosaic Law consisted of three-components:

1.   The Moral Law

These form the heart of God's Law. They are unchanging. They reveal to us the very essence and nature of God and guide all aspects of our life. The core of the Moral Law is the greatest commandment spelled out by Jesus in **Matthew 22:37-40** – *Jesus replied: "'Love the Lord your God with all you heart and with all your soul and with all your mind.' This is the first and the greatest commandment. And the second is like it: 'Love your neighbour as yourself.' All the Law and the Prophets hang on these two commandments."*

2.   The Civil Law

These laws draw from the principles of the Moral Law and translate them into guidelines for everyday living. For example: The Ten Commandments say – *You shall not steal.* This is a moral law. One of the civil laws based on this moral law is – *If a man steals an ox or a sheep and slaughters it or sells it, he must pay back five head of cattle for the ox and four sheep for the sheep.* **(Exodus 22:1)**

Our societies and social structures have changed drastically over the centuries, so many of the ancient civil laws have become redundant. Nonetheless, since they are based upon the enduring Moral Law, they can be adapted to changing times and cultures keeping their inherent principles intact.

3.   The Ceremonial Law

These deal with the various rules and regulations of worshipping God. It outlines the details of various rituals, offerings and sacrifices to be made, holy days and festivals to be observed, etc. The Ceremonial Law was a constant reminder of God's holiness and faithfulness, and God's desire for Israel to be holy.

Whenever Israel observed any of the prescribed festivals, they were to remember God's greatness. The Passover was a reminder of Israel's escape from Egypt. The Feast of Weeks celebrated God's blessings during the harvest. The Feast of Tabernacles celebrated after the completion of threshing reminded Israel of their time in the desert. While these festivals were a reminder of their past hardships, it was an even greater reminder of God's abundant providence and faithfulness. (Ref. **Deuteronomy 16**)

The Ceremonial Law also contained elaborate purification rituals to remind Israel of God's holiness. The Priests and Levites had to follow the highest standards of ritual purity because they ministered before God. Even minor lapses were catastrophic. In **Leviticus 10** we read about Nadab and Abihu, the sons of Aaron. They offered unauthorized fire before the LORD contrary to the command and they died before the LORD. Bible paints a terrifying picture – *So, fire came out from the presence of the LORD and consumed them…*

The Ceremonial Law contained specific guidelines on how to worship God. One of the central features of worship was atonement made through various kinds of sacrifices. These atoning sacrifices were meant to be a painful reminder of the devastating effects of sin. They were also a reminder of God's desire to forgive and restore. They were meant to make Israel repent and live a holy life in obedience to God's commands.

According to the Ceremonial Law, Jesus Christ took upon himself the burden of the sins of all humanity and died as an atoning sacrifice. In rising again, Jesus Christ triumphed over death and evil and made way for us to live a holy life through faith in Him. By living a blameless life, Jesus Christ fulfilled the Law and made certain elements of the Law obsolete.

- Jesus Christ made the Levitical priesthood obsolete. Now, Jesus is our one and only High Priest forever.
- By becoming the once-and-for-all atoning sacrifice for the whole world, Jesus Christ removed all mandated sacrifices and offerings as prescribed in the Law.
- The ceremonial worship was exclusive to Israel. Jesus made way for all peoples and all nations to worship God in spirit and truth. The whole world is God's worship place. People can worship in all tongues. People can approach God directly in the name of Jesus Christ.
- Jesus Christ also removed the penalties associated with various laws. A case in point is the example of

the woman caught in adultery **(John 8).** Jesus forgave her and commanded her to leave her life of sin. According to the Law, the punishment for adultery was death by stoning. *[Note: This does not change the fact that people will continue to be judged and punished according to the various laws of the land.]* When it comes to moral judgements, unlike the Old Testament, now God is the sovereign judge and executioner. Christians are called to love and forgive one another and let God be their avenger.

The Greatest Commandment stands firm and it guides all aspects of a Christian's life. In **Matthew 5:17,19** Jesus says – *Do not think that I have come to abolish the Law or the Prophets; I have not come to abolish them but to fulfil them. Anyone who breaks one of the least of these commandments and teaches others to do the same will be called least in the kingdom of heaven, but whoever practices and teaches these commands will be called great in the kingdom of heaven.*

When we read the Gospels and meditate on the teachings of Jesus Christ, they expound the Moral Law of the Old Testament and teach us that all law is ultimately based on love. When we let God's love rule our hearts, through Jesus Christ and the Holy Spirit, we can live a blameless life before God.

When our faith is based on God's love and grace, our life and worship is transformed. *To put things in perspective:*

- Jesus Christ abolished the Levitical priesthood but he has called each one of us to be his witnesses and saints. We are called to be holy as God is holy; and to love one another just as Christ Jesus loves us. (Ref. **Matthew 5:48; John 15:12)**
- Jesus Christ removed all mandated offerings and sacrifices but we are called to be generous in our

giving. Our giving is no longer mandated but it is inspired by love and grace. (Ref. **Matthew 10:8)**

- We are no longer required to worship only in Jerusalem or facing Jerusalem; or pray according to the prescribed timings. Instead we can worship anywhere, anytime in spirit and truth. (Ref. **John 4:21-24).** We are called to remain in prayer, in constant communion with God so that we do not fall into temptations. (Ref. **Matthew 25:41)**

- Jesus often quoted **Hosea 6:6** – *I desire mercy, not sacrifice.* Jesus Christ has called us to a life of forgiveness, mercy and compassion. We are called to forgive as we have been forgiven, to show mercy as we have been shown mercy, and to have compassion just as God had compassion for us and made way for us through Jesus Christ to be reconciled to Him.

OUR STRUGGLE WITH SIN

So, we now know that God is unchanging and the spirit of God's Law endures forever. As born-again children of God, redeemed through the love and grace of Jesus Christ our Lord, and born of the Holy Spirit, we must not sin anymore. In **Romans 6**, Apostle Paul writes – *Count yourselves dead to sin but alive to God in Christ Jesus. Therefore do not let sin reign in your mortal body so that you obey its evil desires.*

But we know that we sin. **1 John 1:8** says – *If we claim to be without sin, we deceive ourselves and the truth is not in us.*

What a dilemma! On one hand, the Bible tells us that a person who is born-again will not continue to sin; while on the other hand, the Bible also tells us that if we claim to be without sin we are liars. **1 John 3:6** goes on to say that *no one who lives in Christ Jesus keeps on sinning and no one who continues to sin has either seen him or known him.* Does it mean that we have no hope at all? Does it mean that we are just as trapped in sin now as we were before Christ Jesus?

Let's not lose hope and look deeper into what the Bible tells about "sinning". The Law makes us aware of sin. God is just. Jesus knows exactly what we are going through. God knows our heart. He looks into our motives. One of our greatest comforts as well as greatest fears is that God knows everything, even the deepest and darkest secrets of our heart. Nothing is hidden from him. No one can escape him.

When we read the Bible we realize that God is not a tyrant but a merciful God. When God gave the Law He was well aware that people may not be able to fully follow God's very high standards. So, He instated the provision for atonement of sins. The person who had sinned was required to offer a sin offering. An innocent unblemished animal was to take the place of the sinner and die on his behalf to absolve the sinner of his sins. The sin offering was meant to be offered in deep repentance. However, this atonement was not applicable for all kinds of sins. The Word of God tells us about the different kinds of sin or the different ways in which we sin.

VARIOUS WAYS IN WHICH WE MAY SIN

Based on intention and possibility of atonement, the Old Testament Law categorized sins under three broad categories:

A. Unintentional sins

Leviticus 4 and 5 contain a detail description of how a person can commit unintentional sins.

a. Unintentional sins of the whole community (Ref. **Leviticus 4:13-21; Numbers 15:22-26)**
b. Unintentional sin of an individual (Ref. **Leviticus 4:22-35; Leviticus 5:1-13; Numbers 15:27-29)**

Unintentional sins were committed due to ignorance, carelessness or thoughtless. There could be more reasons but the original word for *'unintentionally'* meant *'wandering away'* signifying *'spiritual weakness of human beings'*. Unlike the intentional sins which were committed in outright rebellion, awareness of one's unintentional sins brought remorse and repentance. Therefore, the guilt issuing from unintentional sins could be remedied through sin offerings and guilt offerings.

The elements of the remedy for unintentional sins were:

- **Confession on awareness** – coming out to offer sacrifices to remedy ones sins was itself a sign of confession
- **Penalty** – the prescribed offering for ritual purification
- **Repentance** – a resolve to not commit the same offense again
- **Restitution** – full refund plus 20%

One other important point of note about the remedy for unintentional sins was that the punishment varied according to a person's status. Contrary to the existing practices of the time where influential people could get away even after committing heinous crimes, God's Law held them to higher standards. These people were chosen to lead the masses through their exemplary lives; so they not only failed themselves by sinning, they also led the common people astray. Thus,

- An anointed priest had to offer a young bull without blemish
- A leader had to offer a male goat without defect
- A member of the community had to offer a female goat/lamb without defect

The remedy for unintentional sins in the Old Testament recognized the inherent weakness of the human character. More than ritual cleansing, it was meant to foster spiritual discipline and encourage holy living – honouring God and establishing love amongst each other.

B. Intentional/Defiant sins

These are intentional sins committed 'with a high hand' suggesting blatant disregard for the law and God's authority. There was no remedy for a sinner who had committed sins in defiance because the sinner felt no remorse. It was an open rejection of God's holy covenant. Such sins not only rejected God's authority, they challenged and mocked God. A person who committed sins in defiance was to be *'completely cut-off'*. Defiant sins led to capital punishment i.e. death. **(Ref. Numbers 15:30-31).** In some cases it even led to the termination of the whole family.

C. Mortal sins

According to the Old Testament Law, five categories of violations were dealt with most severely. The punishment for these violations did not consider intention or motive of the defaulter. These five categories of violations defiled God's holiness by taking Him lightly. They demonstrated the offender's irreverence towards God. **Numbers 15:32-36** tells us of a man who was gathering wood on the Sabbath. When Moses consulted God, *the LORD said to Moses, "The man must die. The whole assembly must stone him outside the camp."*

Today it might appear a bit too harsh to us. We may reason that he was just gathering some firewood – it doesn't seem like a big offense. Perhaps there was no malice in his heart. But when we look deeper, it reflects the man's disregard for God. Sabbath was a mandatory day-off for all Israel. There's no way the man was unaware of it. Everyone observed Sabbath so it was hard to miss. Sabbath regulations were spoken of so regularly that it was impossible to be ignorant about it. The Law concerning Sabbath was absolute. Though the act of gathering wood may seem very harmless, the act of breaking Sabbath was defiance. Similar to the Sabbath Law, there were some laws that were considered sacrosanct. No one could claim innocence for breaking them.

"Karat" in Hebrew refers to being cut-off, and it was reserved for five of the most atrocious and blasphemous offenses:

1. Violation of sacred time i.e. neglect of certain holy days.
2. Violation of sacred substances, like consumption of blood
3. Neglect of purification rituals, like circumcision
4. Illicit worship i.e. pagan rituals or idolatry
5. Unlawful sexual relations, like homosexuality, bestiality, etc.

The Old Testament Law required Israel to stay away from evil and pursue good. Therefore, sins could also be categorized as:

A. Sins of Commission

Most of the regulations we read about in the Law tells us about 'what not to do': *Do not steal. Do not commit adultery. Do not give false testimony....* If we ignore them and end up stealing, or committing adultery or lying – we are guilty of the sin of commission. Sins of commission are doing the things we are told not to do.

B. Sins of Omission

However, there are also a number of regulations and commands in the Bible that encourage us to pursue good. In many instances choosing to be self-involved or neutral can also harm others. Sins of omission are all about withholding good. The very first example that springs to my mind is the Greatest Commandment. We are called to actively pursue love – Love God and love one another.

Many a times, we may think it is quite sufficient if I just mind my own business. While we shouldn't unnecessarily poke into other's businesses, the Bible clearly tells us if we do not help others in need, we are guilty. For example – *If a person sins because he does not speak up when he hears a public charge to testify regarding something he has seen or learned about, he will be held responsible.* **(Leviticus 5:1)** Withholding information may have no effect on us but it has power to wrongly let an innocent person suffer.

Another interesting example that struck me is **Deuteronomy 22:8** – *When you build a new house, make a parapet around your roof so that you may not bring the guilt of bloodshed on your house if someone falls from the roof.* In today's world when people dump their garbage into their neighbour's compound without any qualm, I can't help but admire God's Law and be in awe of God's meticulous standards that encourage us to actively pursue good and be mindful of others.

Thus far we have seen quite a lot about the Old Testament Law. If we omit the ceremonial law and penalties for various sins, I find the Law is more advanced than any existing national or international law today. However, does the New Testament contradict any of the Old Testament Moral Law in any way? Does Jesus or any of the apostles contradict the Law in any way?

JESUS RENEWED THE LAW

By the time Jesus came to the world, the spirit of the Law had long been forgotten and people hung on to only the traditions. In **Matthew 23**, Jesus calls out the hypocrisy of the teachers of the Law. Unlike today when we all have our own copies of the Bible, during the time of Jesus Christ on earth the common people did not have their personal copies of the Scriptures. In fact, most people would have been illiterate. Copies of the Scriptures were made available to all the synagogues and the teachers of the Law were responsible for teaching the masses about God's laws and commands. With time the focus had shifted from holy living to mere observation of the ceremonial law. When we meditate on the New Testament, we understand how Jesus Christ transformed and renewed the Law.

A. Jesus' attitude towards the teachers of the Law *versus* the common people

While Jesus often confronted the teachers of the Law and showed them the error of their ways, he showed compassion to the masses. His attitude towards the teachers of the Law shows us that he was well aware of their blatant sins, their false teachings and legalistic ways steeped in human tradition but away from God's ways. They were sinning intentionally and did not feel any remorse even when confronted. Intentional sins or wilful sins are unpardonable even in the New Testament and new way of life through Jesus Christ. We cannot simply defy God's authority and live under the illusion that we have eternal life.

On the other hand, Jesus displayed immense compassion for the common people. **Matthew 9:36** says – *When Jesus saw the crowds, he had compassion on them, because they were harassed and helpless, like sheep without a shepherd.* Jesus spent most of his time teaching them. When we meditate on Jesus' teachings, they are all built upon the Greatest Commandment. He discoursed and explained what the laws demanded of the people. He clarified that the laws didn't demand meaningless rituals and endless sacrifices but to live holy lives. **Matthew 7:12** – *So in everything, do to others what you would have them do to you, for this sums up the Law and the Prophets.* The masses represented unintentional sinners. However, while he freely extended forgiveness to the sinners, he also warned them to not sin again. **John 5:14** tells us – *Later Jesus found him at the temple and said to him, "See, you are well again. Stop sinning or something worse may happen to you."* We cannot persist in sin, even if it is unintentional. We need to continually grow in our spiritual life. We need to give full rein to the Holy Spirit to cleanse and transform us. Persisting in sin eventually makes us disregard God's grace.

B. Jesus' focus on the heart of the Law

Christians often talk of the New Law and the New Command. After all, what is this New Command?

Jesus Christ says in **John 13:34-35** – *A new command I give you: Love one another. As I have loved you, so you must love one another. By this all men will know that you are my disciples, if you love one another.*

Going a step further, in **John 15:9-10** Jesus says – *As the Father has loved me, so have I loved you. Now remain in my love. If you obey my commands, you will remain in my love, just as I have obeyed my Father's commands and remain in his love.*

Aren't these verses built on the Greatest Commandment? Jesus Christ came to this world to show us the way – the right way to love. Jesus showed us the Father's love and calls us to emulate that love. Love and obedience reinforce one another. They are the result of our salvation and they are the sign of our salvation. We no longer obey because of some obligation or law but because we love God and it is the only right thing to do. **1 Corinthians 16:14** summarizes Jesus' teachings perfectly – *Do everything in love.*

Smita Valentina

C. Jesus' references to the Prophets

Jesus reminded the people, including the teachers of the Law, about the prophesies that pointed to him and to the New Covenant. Earlier, Israel had ignored God's Law and the Prophets and continued to rebel against God. Jesus' references to the Prophets was a reminder of Israel's continued unfaithfulness and a final call to repent. After Jesus Christ's atoning sacrifice there is no more sacrifice left for reconciliation. Jesus is our only hope.

Isaiah 6:9-10 (quoted in **Matthew 13:14-15**) –

> *"You will be ever hearing but never understanding;*
> *you will be ever seeing but never perceiving.*
> *For this people's heart has become calloused;*
> *they hardly hear with their ears,*
> *and they have closed their eyes.*
> *Otherwise they might see with their eyes,*
> *hear with their ears,*
> *understand with their hearts*
> *and turn, and I would heal them."*

Isaiah 29:13 (quoted in **Matthew 15:8-9**) –

> *"These people honour me with their lips,*
> *but their hearts are far from me.*
> *They worship me in vain;*
> *their teachings are but rules taught by men."*

Isaiah 61:1-2 (quoted in **Luke 4:18-19**) –

> *"The Spirit of the Lord is on me,*
> *because he has anointed me*
> *to preach good news to the poor.*
> *He has sent me to proclaim freedom for the prisoners*
> *and recovery of sight for the blind,*

> *to release the oppressed,*
> *to proclaim the year of the Lord's favour."*

The many references that Jesus uses in the gospels reflect God's love and willingness to forgive us despite our rebellious sinful nature. At the same time, Jesus also continually reiterates that God is not only willing to forgive us; He has also prepared a way for us to overcome our sinful nature. If we believe in Jesus Christ, repent from our old ways and return to God, He is waiting to welcome us back into His Kingdom as His children.

Jesus also shows us that if we reject God's offer of reconciliation through Jesus Christ, there's no more scope for forgiveness left. The *Parable of the Tenants* is a stark warning.

D. The New Covenant

Luke 22:20 – *In the same way, after the supper he took the cup, saying, "This cup is the new covenant in my blood, which is poured out for you…"*

The Old Covenant was the covenant between God and Israel according to God's promise that He made with Abram. God had chosen to bless Abram and make him a blessing to all the nations around him. Similarly, Israel was chosen by God to be His envoy on earth. God's perfect Covenant Law was to guide them towards holy living and draw other nations to the One true God – the LORD. However, Israel had failed miserably. Not only were they not able to bring other nations to the knowledge of the LORD, they themselves had turned away from God. Despite repeated warnings they continued to revel in their sin.

We see glimpses of God's desire for a new covenant in various prophetic books.

Jeremiah 31:31, 33 – *"The time is coming," declares the LORD, "when I will make a new covenant with the house of Israel and with the house of Judah." "This is the covenant I will make with the house of Israel after that time," declares the LORD. "I will put my law in their minds and write it on their hearts. I will be their God, and they will be my people."*

Ezekiel 36:26-27 – *I will give you a new heart and put a new spirit in you; I will remove from you your heart of stone and give you a heart of flesh. And I will put my Spirit in you and move you to follow my decrees and be careful to keep my laws.*

God has made a New Covenant with the whole world through Jesus Christ – *For God so loved the world that he gave his one and only Son, Jesus Christ, that whoever believes in him shall not perish but have eternal life. For God did not send his Son into the world to condemn the world, but to save the world through him.* **(John 3:16-17)**

This New Covenant is sealed through the blood of Jesus Christ who died for the sins of the whole world as an atoning sacrifice on the Cross. And who rose again on the third day, proclaiming eternal life to all who believe in Him. He defeated sin and death and made way for us to enter into eternal life through Him.

LAW, SIN AND RIGHTEOUSNESS IN THE NEW COVENANT

A. Jesus is the only way to the Father

In **John 14:6** Jesus says – *I am the way and the truth and the life. No one comes to the Father except through me.*

According to the new covenant with Jesus Christ as the sole mediator, there is only one way to forgiveness and eternal life and that is through Jesus. The Old Testament sacrifices for sin and guilt are no longer required and nor are they applicable anymore under the New Covenant.

B. Love is the only Command

In **John 15:12** Jesus says – *My command is this: Love each other as I have loved you.*

The context of this verse gives us the full extent of Jesus' teachings. There are no embellishments. In **John 14:23-24**, Jesus candidly puts it thus – *If anyone loves me, he will obey my teaching. My Father will love him, and we will come to him and make our home with him. He who does not love me will not obey my teaching. These words you hear are not my own; they belong to the Father who sent me.*

According to the New Covenant, Christians are asked to remain in God's love and do everything in love. Our life, our worship, our obedience, our relationship with others… every aspect of our life must be inspired by Christ-like love.

God's love is the foundation of our faith while our demonstration of love through obedience is the expression of our faith. This New Covenant Law of Love is like a blanket law that covers the entirety of the law we are called to obey.

Speaking of our faith in Jesus Christ, **Romans 3:31** says – *Do we, then, nullify the law by this faith? Not at all!!! Rather, we uphold the law.*

C. Jesus Christ is our constant mediator in Heaven

John 17 shows us that Jesus prays for us. He is praying for all believers. Seated at the right-hand of God, Jesus is constantly advocating for us. What a great comfort!

According to the Old Testament law, the High Priest advocated for Israel. **Hebrews** tells us of the transition from the Old Covenant to the New Covenant and the change of priesthood. The Priest offered regular sacrifices for his own sins as well as the sins of the whole assembly of Israel. The priests were replaced regularly because death prevented them from continuing in the office forever. This earthly priest had limited access.

Now, **Hebrews 4:14-16** tells us – *Therefore, since we have a great high priest who has gone through the heavens, Jesus the Son of God, let us hold firmly to the faith we profess. For we do not have a high priest who is unable to sympathize with our weaknesses, but we have one who has been tempted in every way, just as we are – yet was without sin. Let us then approach the throne of grace with confidence, so that we may receive mercy and find grace to help us in our time of need.*

Further, speaking of Jesus Christ as the permanent High Priest, **Hebrews 8:1-2** says – *We do have such a high priest, who sat down at the right hand of the throne of the Majesty in heaven, and who serves in the sanctuary, the true tabernacle set up by the Lord, not by man.*

According to the New Testament, Jesus Christ is the permanent and perfect High Priest of the New Covenant.

D. Holy Spirit is our Counsellor

God knows our weaknesses and He sympathizes with them. He knows that we are too weak to overcome the temptations of this world alone despite the gift of grace. Therefore, Jesus promised the Holy Spirit to all who believe in him. The Holy Spirit empowers us to remain in Christ Jesus.

First, in **John 14:15** Jesus says – *"If you love me, you will obey what I command. And I will ask the Father, and he will give you another Counsellor to be with you forever."* Again in **John 14:26**, Jesus says – *"But the Counsellor, the Holy Spirit, whom the Father will send in my name, will teach you all things and will remind you of everything I have said to you."*

The Apostles and early disciples who received the Holy Spirit and experienced His transformative power have written extensively about it in the Acts of the Apostles and various epistles of the New Testament.

Acts 1:8 quotes Jesus' commission to the disciples – *But you will receive power when the Holy Spirit comes on you; and you will be my witnesses in Jerusalem, and in all Judea and Samaria, and to the ends of the earth.*

This was fulfilled on the day of Pentecost when the Holy Spirit filled the disciples and they began manifesting great signs and wonders and above all, a transformed life. (Ref. **Acts 2** onwards)

In the Old Testament, God filled certain selected people with the Holy Spirit temporarily for certain appointed tasks. According to the New Covenant, the Holy Spirit remains with all those who believe, forever; continuing the sanctification work in our lives till we are made perfect.

E. Jesus, our Righteousness

Earlier I had used 'Lighthouse' as a metaphor for the Law. Thus far, we have seen and we all agree that the Law is good and perfect. We also agree that we sin even though we are born again. Then, how come we become blameless before God through Jesus Christ.

2 Corinthians 5:21 says – *God made him who had no sin to be sin for us, so that in him we might become the righteousness of God.*

Here, I would like to elaborate on that 'Lighthouse' metaphor:

The Law is the lighthouse. The moral requirements of the Law are unchanging. The ceremonial requirements of the Law have been fulfilled by Jesus Christ. So, as we are struggling to attain the righteousness that God demands of us; Jesus has defeated sin and death and he knows the way. In fact, he is the only way because he is the only One who has made that journey. He came from heaven to earth to show us the way, he took upon himself the sins of the whole world, he died and rose again defeating sin and death, and he is now seated on the right-hand of God, the Father.

Imagine now: In the world of darkness when it is quite easy for us to miss the light of the Lighthouse, Jesus has come with an infallible ship. He calls to all who hear and believe in him – *Hop on… Trust me… I know the way… Don't bother about the darkness; in fact, I can take you to eternal life safely blindfolded because I am the way. Holy Spirit will be your helper and counsellor. It's going to be a challenging journey but you let the Holy Spirit take care of you and everything will be fine.* When we trust in Jesus and believe in him, we accept his offer of salvation and choose to follow him.

We are called to come just as we are. But most of us are unsure of the journey and we come aboard with plenty of baggage. Interestingly, there's no inspection as we enter. There aren't many rules. The Holy Spirit reminds us Jesus' words from the Gospels – When we had decided to board Jesus' ship we had made the commitment to follow Jesus. We had accepted Jesus as our personal Saviour, Lord and God; and we had decided to obey Jesus' commands. Jesus' command had appeared quite simple: *Love one another as I have loved you.* Eventually, our baggage begins bothering us. Holy Spirit tells us – *Why are you still holding this grudge against your brother? Let it go. Forgive as you were forgiven and your burden will lighten.* It is still difficult for me to forgive. Holy Spirit is quite persistent – *Let me remind you what you were, He says. Were you very holy? Yet Jesus forgave you. Now you are called to extend that same compassion towards your brother. Remember God's love for you and it will be easier.* It takes time but gradually I realize I am letting go of that grudge and I feel lighter.

As we board the ship, we realize it is not a five-star cruise. Jesus reminds us – *I told you, in this world you will have trouble.*

We are tossed around in the sea as waves crash against the ship. We feel homesick. We feel sea-sick. At times we have insufficient food and inadequate clothing. We hurt. We long to just return. Jesus keeps encouraging us: *Just a while longer. We are almost there. You will no longer hunger or thirst. You will no more be in pain or shame or sickness.* We must hold on. But we see many abandoning the ship midway. They just jump into the dark abyss ignoring Jesus' promises and refusing to let the Holy Spirit take control of their situation.

I find a corner and hide myself. I read the Bible. It comforts me. I pray to God for strength to hold on. Holy Spirit comes and points towards another passenger who appears to be going through tough time – *Why don't you go and spend some time with her? She is contemplating abandoning the ship.* I retaliate – *I don't even know her.* Holy Spirit persists – *How do you show God's love to others if you sit in one corner!* I still hesitate – *What will I say, I have no idea?* Holy Spirit encourages – *Don't worry. I will teach you what you must say.* I go to her. I feel a bit reluctant. I don't know whether she wants to even talk to me. But soon we are sharing our burdens with one another, singing joyfully and the journey starts feeling more bearable.

I realise that I am noticing things I never noticed earlier. God's love is welling within me. I can now encourage others more easily. I can share more generously. I can forgive more graciously.

It is not just us; everyone in this world has an awareness and yearning for eternal life. Everyone is trying to attain it according to their own ways and understanding. So, as we set sail with Jesus on the helm, we also see other ships trying to reach the Kingdom of Heaven. They are quite attractive. Many have modern fittings. Many have exceptional entertainment options. The passengers aboard those ships look quite comfortable. These ships look quite sturdy –

Smita Valentina

unshakable and unsinkable. Many those who are with us begin ogling at the glittering ships that pass by us.

I too steal a glance now and then. Sometimes I feel envious. Holy Spirit points out – *They look happy but are they really happy! Look, as they retire to their rooms at night, you can see sorrow written across their faces.* I look at this one ship that is sailing quite close to us. The Holy Spirit encourages me to bring them over to our ship. I am apprehensive – *Will they leave the comfort of their luxury ship and come aboard our battered one?* The Holy Spirit reasons – *What's the harm in trying! Doesn't Jesus tell that we must love our enemies also!* It's a conundrum but I know I must at least try. I am not too worried now because the Holy Spirit is with me all the time. I smile and wave. The passenger on the other ship is pleasantly surprised. I tell him about Jesus and how coming aboard our ship is the only way to Heaven. He is torn between the investment he has made to get a seat in his splendid ship and his desire to reach heaven. He wants more time to think over it. He asks me to come aboard his ship so he could learn more. For a while, I am tempted. Thankfully, the Holy Spirit protects me from the trap. *What was I about to do! Abandon Jesus' ship! How foolish of me!* I look around and see. Almost everyone in our ship is trying to win over the passengers from other ships. Many are falling into the trap of the evil and ignoring Holy Spirit as they change ship. They reason it is only for a while to win over the other passengers to our ship. But eventually, we notice, they remain stuck in those other doomed ships. We try to bring them back but they throw world philosophies at us – *All roads lead to God,* they say. Some say, *there's no God, there's only science. There's no heaven.*

Those who had thus far been passive are now struggling with spiritual weaknesses. They are noticing the confusion around. Many are contemplating changing the ship. Jesus and the Holy Spirit plead with them not to abandon our ship. *Narrow is the way that leads to the Kingdom of God.* But some are almost on the verge of giving up – *Why do the wicked prosper while the righteous suffer, they ask? See, they do not suffer any lack. Here we are sacrificing everything for others each day.* Jesus answers – *You are storing up treasures in heaven.* As we are nearing the end of our journey, each hour we are struggling more and more. Our struggle in preventing our fellow passengers from abandoning Jesus' ship is much greater than bringing others aboard.

As we sail ahead, still tossed about – we hear crashes around us. Many are abandoning their luxury ships and trying to get to our ship. For once, we think that Jesus won't let them come aboard. But he welcomes them graciously. Now some of us mutter even more – *Is it fair? They were enjoying so far while we were struggling and now we have to share everything with these pathetic sinners.* Jesus says compassionately – *Do not let your hearts be troubled. Trust in God; trust also in me. In my Father's house are many rooms.*

We can see the pearly gates of Heaven now. It has been an arduous journey but we have made it. As we are about to reach, we notice that a number of ships are waiting to enter. The passengers aboard those ships are being investigated. Many of them appear to be begging. As Jesus' ship reaches the harbour, the pearly gates open for us. We enter without any inspection. We notice that all the angels are bowing before Jesus and giving praises to him. The gates shut behind us. In contrast to the darkness of the world, the Heaven is so bright that every one of us gets bathed in its brightness. When we look at ourselves and our fellow passengers, we are all transformed. Now we have a glorified body. We ask Jesus – *What about all those other ships in the harbour?* Jesus replies – *I told you, no one comes to the Father except through me.*

****

Smita Valentina

For a very long time I was struggling to come up with an illustration that can explain our journey to eternal life by faith in Jesus Christ. Some concepts that we discuss intellectually are too difficult for everyone to grasp. One such concept is "how Jesus' righteousness is imputed on those who believe in him". As I was praying and pondering over it, the Holy Spirit placed this beautiful illustration in my mind. The moment I framed this illustration, I was amazed at how many questions this illustration answers.

Our faith journey is a journey of continuous cleansing and transformation. Let us always remember that Jesus is our righteousness and Holy Spirit is our constant Counsellor. Let the Holy Spirit perfect the work of salvation in your life and cling to Jesus for only he can lead us to Heaven.

THE LAW WRITTEN IN OUR HEARTS

We have discussed quite a lot about Law and Sin. I hope you have gained more clarity in your understanding of these vital truths that are foundational to our Christian faith. So, in my concluding remarks, I thought I would share with you one final insight.

One day when I was meditating on the Word of God, a thought occurred to me:

The Mosaic Law came into existence only from the Book of Exodus onwards when Israel was in the desert. Before that, from Adam to Noah till all the other generations of people, was there any law in existence? If there was no law, how could God hold the people accountable? If there was no law, how could God destroy the whole earth by flood? How could God destroy Sodom and Gomorrah? If you look at the account presented in Genesis as well as the account of other nations throughout the first five books of the Bible, you may start questioning the fairness of God!

In fact, this is a question raised by many who do not have a living relationship with God and who do not spend time with the Word of God – If there is a God, why is he so whimsical?

The Holy Spirit enlightened me – *Do you remember the first time you felt that you had done something wrong?* I tried to remember. I am sure I would have made mistakes even before this incident, but I recalled one event when I was about five. I found some coins on the table and took them. Then I went to a nearby store and bought gum. I recall I even dragged around my 2 year old sister with me. When I saw my mother looking for the coins I recall becoming acutely aware that I had made many mistakes. I had stolen the money. I had left home without permission. I had bought gum which we were not allowed to chew. I had taken my sister along and also fed her gum. At that age, I did not know what Law was. I did not even know God personally. When I recalled this, I realized God has put His Law in each one of our hearts.

This clarifies a number of doubts, such as:

- There are people who do not know about Jesus and yet they are good. They may not be perfect but many are much better than namesake Christians.
- Why is there a universal agreement that certain deeds, like murder, are evil?
- Why is there a universal agreement about the merit of good deeds like helping the needy?
- Why do we feel guilty and ashamed even when we claim we haven't done anything wrong? Example – A young boy or girl trying to smoke a cigarette. When we are in a wrong relationship...

The Holy Spirit took me to the creation of Adam and Eve. **Genesis 1:26** tells us that *God made us in His own image and* *likeness.* What is this *'image and likeness'*? Doesn't it encompass the nature and qualities of God! Doesn't God's Law tell us about His nature and qualities!

Romans 1:18 clarifies it further – *The wrath of God is being revealed from heaven against all the godlessness and wickedness of men who suppress the truth by their wickedness, since what may be known about God is plain to them, because God has made it plain to them. For since the creation of the world God's invisible qualities – his eternal power and divine nature – have been clearly seen, being understood from what has been made, so that men are without excuse.*

God had put His perfect Law in the heart of all mankind but we had continuously chosen to ignore that Law. God's punishment was His wrath against our outright rebellion. Our hearts had imbibed so much evil that they could no longer discern right from wrong. The Mosaic Law attempted to make us conscious of our sins but it depended so much on human mediation through the Levitical priesthood and human will to obey that it could not make us stop sinning. Throughout the Prophets we witness God's desire to *"change our hearts of stone and give us a new heart of flesh"*. God says, *"I will put my law in their minds and write it on their hearts..."* God says, *"I will give them an undivided heart and put a new spirit in them..."*

Romans 2:13-15 says – *For it is not those who hear the law who are righteous in God's sight, but it is those who obey the law who will be declared righteous. (Indeed, when Gentiles, who do not have the law, do by nature things required by the law, they are a law for themselves, even though they do not have the law, since they show that the requirements of the law are written on their hearts, their consciences also bearing witness, and their thoughts now accusing, now even defending them.)*

Finally, in the New Covenant we find the perfect and permanent mediation through Jesus Christ, our Saviour and

High Priest; and, the Holy Spirit, our Counsellor to constantly remind us of God's Law written in our hearts and empower us to live in obedience to God's Law.

Moses spoke to Israel (**Deuteronomy 30:11-14**):

Now what I am commanding you today is not too difficult for you or beyond your reach. It is not up in the heaven, so that you have to ask, "Who will ascend into heaven to get it and proclaim it to us so we may obey it?" Nor is it beyond the sea, so that you have to ask, "Who will cross the sea to get it and proclaim it to us so we may obey it?" No, the word is very near you; it is in your mouth and in your heart so you may obey it.

How much more significant it is for us today to carry God's Law in our hearts when we are Jesus Christ's witnesses on earth. As you read this, I challenge you:

"You show that you are a letter from Christ… written not with ink but with the Spirit of the Living God, not on tablets of stone but on tablets of human hearts." (**2 Corinthians 3:3**)

****

Smita Valentina

II

SIN & GUILT

Sin & Guilt

Smita Valentina

II

We are like nomads. My husband is a project consultant and we have to frequently change houses because of his transfers. For me, the biggest challenge is packing and unpacking. As I begin sorting through our stuff, very soon I realize how much clutter we have gathered. We are not impulse buyers but we have a tendency to hold on to old things longer than we should. There are piles of old clothes that cannot even be given away but they are stuffed in the bottom shelf of our wardrobe because I want to use them as dusters or make pot-holders out of them. I have been too busy with my work that I did not find time to finish that project and now I am struggling with the dilemma of whether I should just discard them or carry them along to our next home.

As my de-cluttering progresses I realize many of our quarrels were futile. I had often complained that there was no space to keep stuff but I had kept the space occupied with clutter. My husband had disapproved of me buying that other cabinet but I had fumed – *You don't know how I arrange things at home. I can't leave everything piled up in our guest bedroom.* If only I had de-cluttered earlier, we would never have argued about space or the other cabinet.

We move to our next home. As I unpack I notice that I have simply been carrying certain boxes from one location to another without even unpacking them. I have even forgotten what's in some of them. I contemplate whether I should unpack them. I reason – *If I haven't used them in a long time may be I don't need to use them now. But, since I have kept them they must be valuable.* I don't have the heart to open those sealed boxes and I just put them in my bed's box-storage. A few transfers later, I finally open a few of them and find beautiful tableware. But lo! The shock of multiple journeys has made them more fragile. A few of them crack while rinsing. Now, I tear the packaging one after the other and I am flabbergasted at the unnecessary load I had been carrying over the years without even realizing it.

Guilt is at times like that clutter which bothers us even when we are unaware of its source. When we have a narrow understanding of God's Law and Sin, we may continue in practices that may appear good to us but are, in truth, sinful ways. Sometimes, even our cherished habits may be useless for our spiritual growth and they end up taking a lot of our time and effort. And, quite often, our struggle with guilt stems out of the clutter of our spiritual weaknesses that we leave unaddressed.

We all struggle from guilt at some point or the other. Sometimes, the burdens of our past creep up on us in the moments we least expect them, and they overwhelm us with guilt and shame. At other times, guilt gnaws at us from within even though we are clueless about anything wrong that we might have done.

In the previous section we discussed about God's Law and Sin. In this section, we are going to look into the Christian struggle with sin as we pursue holiness. We will try to understand: How we usually respond to sin? What are the various ways in which we express guilt? What should be our Christian response to sin and guilt? What are the ways in which we may continue in sin even after we are born-again? Why do we continue in sin and how can we overcome sin and guilt?

THE MANY EXPRESSIONS OF GUILT

In the Bible we come across many 'expressions' of guilt. One of my most relatable feelings of guilt can be found in **Psalm 32:3-5**,

When I kept silent, my bones wasted away through my groaning all day long.
For day and night your hand was heavy upon me;
my strength was sapped as in the heat of summer.
Then I acknowledged my sin to you and did not cover up my iniquity.
I said, "I will confess my transgressions to the LORD" –
and you forgave the guilt of my sin.

In many of King David's Psalms we find him speaking about *'guilt'*, which give us an idea of how guilt feels:

- *Guilt feels like a burden too heavy to bear.* **(Psalm 38:4)**
- *Guilt feels like a sickness.* **(Psalm 41:4)**
- *Guilt takes away the joy of salvation.* **(Psalm 51)**
- *Guilt distances us from God's presence.* **(Psalm 51)**

Guilt, in effect, is absence of peace with God. When we are not at peace with God, our hearts condemn us and we cannot come before God with full confidence. (Ref. **1 John 3**)

Almost everyone may experience guilt at some point or the other in their life because it is based on an awareness of a higher power that knows us in and out. Even atheists experience moral dilemma. For born-again Christians, we experience guilt when we sin, intentionally as well as unintentionally, because we know that nothing is hidden from God. We usually associate *'guilt'* with remorse and repentance. This may lead us into assuming that we instinctively feel guilty whenever we sin. However, this is far from the truth.

Contrary to our assumption that the realization of our sins cause remorse and repentance; people respond to this realization in a number of ways depending on their spiritual condition. Guilt isn't a very straightforward feeling. It has a tendency of masking itself in a variety of seemingly disparate feelings and emotions.

Let us look at some instances from the Bible to understand how we may be experiencing and expressing guilt:

a. Adam and Eve (Genesis 3)

When Adam and Eve disobeyed God in the Garden of Eden, they realized they had done something wrong. We see this realization dawn on them as they saw their own nakedness and experienced shame. They tried to cover themselves up and hide from God. When God called them, Adam answered – *I heard you in the garden, and I was afraid because I was naked; so I hid.*

Adam's first response seems to be *fear*. While Adam and Eve's *shame* appears to be related to physical nakedness; it could also be a response to their spiritual failure.

From the account of Adam and Eve's first sin we get to learn a lot about how we tend to respond to the realization of sin:

- First, we may feel afraid of being exposed and ashamed of our sin.
- Second, we may attempt to hide it.
- Third, when we realise that we cannot hide, we are filled with fear.
- Fourth, when confronted we try to defend ourselves instead of admitting our sin.

b. Cain (Genesis 4)

Cain did something wrong. Or perhaps, he was yet to do anything wrong but evil was brewing in his heart. When he offered a sacrifice to God, his offering was not acceptable before God. Rejection of Cain's offering did not make him evaluate himself or feel remorse; instead, Cain's first response was *anger*. God confronted him and even warned Cain that he must master sin that has the power to consume him.

Shortly afterwards, Cain murdered his brother, Abel. Again, when confronted by God, Cain tried to deny and hide his sinful action. He not only demonstrated absolute apathy for his own brother; we also witness his self-involvement. Not once did Cain express remorse.

In **Matthew 5:21-22**, Jesus says – *You have heard that it was said to the people long ago, 'Do not murder, and anyone who murders will be subject to judgement.' But I tell you that anyone who is angry with his brother will be subject to judgement.*

Ephesians 4:26-27 elaborates on the vice of anger – *"In your anger do not sin": Do not let the sun go down while you are still angry, and do not give the devil a foothold.*

Cain suffered from the spiritual weakness (sin) of anger. This led him to sin. At the same time, Cain expressed his guilt as anger and resentment. Perhaps he was angry with himself but he projected it on his brother. Instead of examining himself, he resented his brother and murdered him.

c. King David (2 Samuel 11-12)

In the spring, at a time when kings go off to war and the Israelite army was also at war in Rabbah; David remained in Jerusalem. One evening he saw Bathsheba bathing and lusted after her. Knowing quite well that she was a married woman, David sent messengers to get her and he slept with her. When Bathsheba got pregnant, David realized that his adultery would now be exposed. So, he began plotting ways to hide his sin.

He called for Uriah, Bathsheba's husband, from the battlefield and tried to send him to his wife. David even got Uriah drunk. And when he failed in his attempts to make Uriah sleep with Bathsheba, David got him murdered in the line of war. Then, he made Bathsheba his wife. From the verge of being exposed as an adulterer, David elevated himself in the eyes of the people as a noble person who took a pregnant widow under his protection. However, when Prophet Nathan rebuked David, he confessed his sin and repented.

David was *a man after God's own heart*. In his many Psalms, we notice David's remorse. However, even in David's case we observe that remorse and repentance were not his straightforward responses to sin and guilt. It is scary how far people can go to hide their sin and shame.

It is the sinful human nature that prevents us from confessing our sins. Un-confessed and un-forgiven sins cause guilt. Though we might be overwhelmed with guilt in our heart, we try our best to hide our follies and justify ourselves. While it can protect us from public shame, it cannot restore to us the joy of God's salvation. Our deceptive plans and justifications cannot deceive God. Some of the ways in which we may experience and express 'guilt' are:

i.   **Shame**

Though the Bible tells us to please God rather than please people; it is our nature to seek the approval of people in everything we do. Therefore, when we do something that

Smita Valentina

people will disapprove of, we feel ashamed. Normally, we try to hide our wrongdoings. If we feel that others know of our secret sins, we start avoiding them. Christians, who experience guilt as shame and are unable to repent, may stop being part of a church. Though we can hide from people, we cannot hide from God or ourselves. Shame can make us neglect our personal relationship with God and push us deeper into sin.

ii.   Fear

Adam's response to his sin was fear. What was he afraid of? Perhaps he was afraid of what God would say and do. Maybe he was afraid that his nakedness would be exposed. Cain's panic when God punished him was his fear of retribution – *whoever finds me will kill me.* Fear is usually associated with punishment. However, punishment can take many forms. It can range from social boycott, verbal reprimand, fine or penalties to even physical ones like whipping, imprisonment and death penalty. Often people can withdraw and hide due to fear of punishment. Fear also cuts us off from enjoying a living relationship with God and God's people.

iii.   Denial

After Cain killed his brother Abel, God asked him where his brother was. Cain replied – *I don't know. Am I my brother's keeper?* Did Cain really not know? There are times we do not respect our parents. We shout at them. We get annoyed at them because they don't know how to use modern gadgets. When someone points out to us that we ought to honour our parents, we deny that we have ever been disrespectful to our parents. We may say that we did it out of love and not disrespect. Denial makes us un-teachable. If we do not learn to accept our weakness we will continue repeating our sins and move away from God's presence.

iv.   Rationalization

Denial and rationalization go hand in hand. Adam did not deny eating the forbidden fruit but he tried justifying his action by blaming it on Eve. Often, when we sin and when we are caught, we try to give an excuse. When we don't finish our assignment, we may give an excuse that we were sick or some family emergency cropped up and it may be admissible. It's different with sin. With sin, it does not matter how we did it; all that matters is we sinned. By trying to justify our sinning, we only tighten the noose around our neck. It is based on self-righteousness and it leads to grave spiritual sins.

v.   Anger

In a way, when we sin, it is only natural to be angry at oneself for being careless or ignorant or weak. However, this anger shouldn't consume us. Unfortunately, out of a guilty conscience we start projecting our anger at others. In Cain's case, he resented his brother for his personal shortcomings. When we feel that we cannot deny or justify our sin, we begin lashing out at those who confront us or those who are better than us and make us look bad. Jealousy is anger's twin sister. Anger, in itself, is a spiritual sin. It is also a sign of serious spiritual weakness. Left unchecked it can not only stunt our spiritual growth, but it can also make us lose our salvation.

THE CHRISTIAN RESPONSE TO SIN AND GUILT

Christians are called to live a holy life in obedience to God. We are called to be watchful so that we do not fall into temptations and sin. At the same time, God knows our every weakness; therefore we have Jesus as our advocate and mediator. Whenever we sin, we must repent and be reconciled with God. (Ref. **1 John 2:1-2**)

Smita Valentina

The Christian response to sin and guilt ought to be – **godly sorrow and repentance that brings life.** However, our inability to recognize sins in our life and our inability to understand guilt can be a major road-block in our repentance and reconciliation.

In the previous section of this book, we discussed at length about God's Law and Sin. Drawing from there and various examples from the Bible; let us discuss the ways in which we may sin even after we are born again and the types of guilt we may experience. *(**Please note:** These are not standardized classifications. These are my personal classifications as they enable me to understand 'sin and guilt' better.)*

Few years ago, a young medical student asked me – *Why do I still feel guilty even after seeking forgiveness for my wrongs?* This is a question that must have haunted us as well. Even though the Bible assures us that God has forgiven and forgotten our sins, why does guilt keep following us around?

1 John 3:16-22 gives a picture of what guilt can do to us:

> [16]*This is how we know what love is: Jesus Christ laid down his life for us. And we ought to lay down our lives for our brothers.* [17]*If anyone has material possessions and sees his brother in need but has no pity on him, how can the love of God be in him?* [18]*Dear children, let us not love with words or tongue but with actions and in truth.* [19]***This then is how we know that we belong to the truth, and how we set our hearts at rest in his presence*** [20]***whenever our hearts condemn us. For God is greater than our hearts, and he knows everything.*** [21]***Dear friends, if our hearts do not condemn us, we have confidence before God*** [22]*and receive from him anything we ask, because we obey his commands and do what pleases him.*

Guilt, for a Christian, can cause deep unrest and a burdened heart that condemns us. At the outset, *guilt can rob us of our joy in Christ Jesus* and *disable us from demonstrating*

Christ-like love in our lives. It may also *prevent us from doing the good works* that God has prepared in advance for us to do. If left unchecked, persistent *guilt can affect our confidence in our prayers* and even *challenge our assurance of salvation.*

What's more challenging about guilt is: *An absence of guilt does not necessarily mean that we are sin-free; and, presence of guilt does not always mean that we have sinned.* Guilt is, ultimately, a moral emotion of feeling responsible or regretful for a perceived offence, real or imaginary, concerning violation of certain moral standards, personal or universal. We all have different levels of moral standards and awareness. Our repertoire of moral values encompasses the whole range of values one encounters throughout their life. We learn our values from our family, our society, our religion, our education and much more.

For a Christian, the moral standard is the Word of God and the counsel of the Holy Spirit. The Holy Spirit convicts us whenever we sin so that we come to repentance. The Holy Spirit convicts us even before we commit a sin, unintentionally or intentionally, so that we do not sin. The Holy Spirit also convicts us when we have sinned unintentionally or succumbed to our spiritual weakness and sinned intentionally so that we experience godly sorrow and repent. This is the **righteous guilt** brought upon us by the working of the Holy Spirit and it brings salvation.

At the same time, the Devil can also bring guilt upon us by making us doubt our position in Christ Jesus. The Devil can continually remind us of our past sins and our unworthiness. It can torment us grievously even for minor lapses and weaknesses and make us doubt our self-worth. The Devil can fill us with shame and prevent us from experiencing the complete joy of our salvation. This is **toxic guilt** and it can even cost us our salvation.

Smita Valentina

2 Corinthians 7:10 says – *Godly sorrow brings repentance that leads to salvation and leaves no regret, but worldly sorrow brings death.*

THE SOURCE OF GUILT

The first step towards overcoming guilt is identifying its source. Guilt is our internal moral compass. Usually, when we experience guilt, we have done something wrong. However, we may not always understand the source of our guilt.

Before I accepted Jesus Christ as my personal Saviour, I used to think that I was a very righteous person. When I accepted Jesus Christ as my personal Saviour, I became aware of my unworthiness and sinful state. However, it was only gradually that I became aware of the wrongs I had done. Many a times I reflect upon my childhood days as an elder sister and realize that I failed my sister so miserably multiple times. I wish that I could do it over again. But when I shared this with my sister, strangely enough, I found that she considered me a good sister. It came as a surprise. I realize that now as I am slowly drawing nearer to God each day, my personal moral standards are becoming higher than what it used to be. I am glad my younger sister understands that I was also a child not much older than herself.

The Bible says that the law of the LORD is perfect **(Psalm 19:7)** and through the law we become aware of our sins **(Romans 3:20)**. The more we grow in the knowledge of God's Word, the more we become aware of God's standards. At the same time, through the Holy Spirit we become empowered to overcome sins and guilt in our everyday life. When I tried to understand 'guilt' more deeply, I realized that guilt can come from God as well as from the Devil.

Righteous Guilt

Righteous Guilt or **Godly sorrow** comes when the Holy Spirit convicts us. Jesus says in **John 16:8** – *When he (Holy Spirit) comes, he will convict the world of guilt in regard to sin and righteousness and judgement.*

Though the law is perfect, our knowledge and understanding of the law is imperfect. We may be committing sins due to our lack of proper understanding of God's Law or due to our various spiritual weaknesses.

We have crucified our sinful nature by accepting Jesus Christ in our lives. However, while on earth in our physical bodies, we will continue to struggle with sins. That does not mean sin will overpower us. On the contrary, through the power of the Holy Spirit we are more than conquerors. **Romans 12:21** encourages us – *Do not be overcome by evil, but overcome evil with good.*

Let us look at the various ways in which we may sin for which the Holy Spirit will convict us:

UNINTENTIONAL SINS

These are the sins we commit out of ignorance, arrogance, carelessness or habit.

a.   Ignorant Sins or Sins of Ignorance

In the Old Testament we read of unintentional sins about which the whole Israel was unaware of. (Ref. **Numbers 15:24**) When Abram lied to Pharaoh about Sarai saying that she was his sister, he sinned. However, we can consider it a sin of ignorance because God had not yet given His written law. Perhaps this deceit was quite entrenched in the culture of Abram's time for we see him repeat the same later with Abimelech. Even Isaac lied about Rebekah.

Smita Valentina

Sins of Ignorance occur when we are not aware of a rule or a law that we must obey. The Bible encourages us to gain knowledge. Sins committed in ignorance may be unintentional but when we continue to choose ignorance over knowledge, we will be guilty of despising God.

b. Arrogant Sins or Sins of Arrogance

Sins of arrogance are committed out of pride. When we consider ourselves better than others – physically, morally, spiritually, intellectually, financially, socially – we can become show-offs. We may verbally attribute our superior position to God's grace but our attitude and behaviour will reflect otherwise – *Yes, God has blessed me so richly because I have been faithful.* This kind of attitude is wrong. It propagates the wrong idea that others are not fortunate because they are faithless. It also starts shifting the focus from grace to one's own merit. When we become arrogant, no matter how gifted we are, instead of building others up with our gifts and talents, we may tear others down. There's a thin line between righteousness and self-righteousness. That line is 'self' or 'ego' or 'pride'. If we are not careful, we may very easily put others down, create divisions in congregations and cause infant believers to stumble.

2 Kings 20 tells us about King Hezekiah. God had blessed him abundantly in every way. But he became proud and showed-off his treasures to envoys from Babylon. This displeased God and Prophet Isaiah reprimanded Hezekiah. Ultimately, Hezekiah accepted his guilt and confessed – *The Word of the LORD you have spoken is good.*

c. Inadvertent Sins or Sins of Carelessness

I call this way of sinning, inadvertent, because they are committed carelessly without thinking. They are committed in the heat of the moment. If we only take a pause and think before acting, they can easily be averted.

King David did not give much thought when he lusted after Bathsheba and slept with her. His adultery with Bathsheba covers so many intentional and unintentional sins. King David had achieved almost everything by then. Usually, he led his army in war but this time he chose to stay back in Jerusalem. Though the Law forbid kings to take many wives, influenced by the neighbouring cultures, King David had already begun practising polygamy. Enamoured by Bathsheba, perhaps he first wanted to include her in his harem. When he found out that she was married to Uriah, one of his mighty men, he did not stop lusting. Perhaps, now established as a mighty King, he considered himself above the Law for in most kingdoms, the King was the Law. However, Bathsheba became pregnant and he panicked. We know that David loved the LORD. His adultery with Bathsheba was a momentary lapse of judgement and probably, he had thought he could get away with it. No other king in the neighbouring kingdoms would have felt any guilt whatsoever for sleeping with a beautiful woman and killing her husband (refer *Abraham's fear regarding Sarah's beauty*). But David was no ordinary king. His response wasn't great. He schemed and got Uriah killed. His adultery may have been an act of momentary passion but Uriah's planned murder was a grievous intentional sin.

d. Casual Sins or Sins of Habit

Casual sins are like petty offences that have become so engrained in our lifestyle that we do not even realize we are sinning. Mind you, 'petty offenses' are like tiny darts. They may not always hit someone and injure them grievously; but they have the potential to inflict deep wounds.

Romans 1:28-32 talks about *'what ought not to be done'*. As I read the list, I realized most of us indulge in these vices – greed, depravity, envy, deceit, malice, gossip, slander, insolence, arrogance, boastfulness, disobeying parents, senseless, faithless, heartless, ruthless… **v.32** says – *Although* *they know God's righteous decree that those who do such things deserve death, they not only continue to do these very things but also approve of those who practice them.* Our casual sins prevent us from forming healthy habits of godliness and growing in our spiritual maturity.

INTENTIONAL SINS

These are the sins we commit with full knowledge. We are completely aware of our wrong actions, nevertheless we still do them.

a. Sins of Spiritual Weakness

All our unintentional sins are a sign of spiritual weakness. However, sins of spiritual weakness are those sins where we succumb to the weakness or desires of the flesh because of spiritual indiscipline.

For example – *When we haven't managed to study well for an important exam, often we may panic just before the exam. We had been undisciplined throughout the semester knowing fully well how important the exam is. But on the eve of the exam we begin dreading the consequences of our failure. We pray and try to study as much as possible. It is difficult to concentrate with all the negative thoughts. That's when evil starts brewing in our heart – There is no other option. If you want to pass, you must cheat. We struggle with the dilemma and ultimately, succumb to the fear of failure.*

Intentional sins are thought-out sins. King David had an adulterous affair with Bathsheba in the heat of the moment; but he schemed to hide this adulterous affair, getting Uriah murdered in the process. This was his sin of spiritual weakness. This kind of sin causes the greatest amount of guilt in a born-again Christian. The guilt arising out of this can consume us if we do not surrender to the Holy

Spirit and find our way back to God. Judas Iscariot is the perfect example of someone struggling with spiritual weakness. He was one of the Twelve disciples of Jesus Christ. Even amongst the Twelve, he held a significant position. But out of greed he betrayed Jesus. When realization of his evil deed dawned on Judas, he was filled with remorse. He tried to return the thirty silver coins to the chief priests and the elders who refused to accept the money. He confessed his sin to the wrong people, who condemned him. Ultimately, Judas threw the money into the temple and hanged himself. (Ref. **Matthew 27:1-5)**

Sometimes I ponder, what if Judas had confessed his sin to Jesus instead of confessing to the chief priest and the elders.

Romans 7:14-20 speaks about this spiritual weakness that causes us to sin.

We know that the law is spiritual; but I am unspiritual, sold as a slave to sin. I do not understand what I do. For what I want to do I do not do, but what I hate I do. And if I do what I do not want to do, I agree that the law is good. As it is, it is no longer I myself who do it, but it is sin living in me. I know that nothing good lives in me, that is, in my sinful nature. For I have the desire to do what is good, but I cannot carry it out. For I what I do is not the good I want to do; no, the evil I do not want to do – this I keep on doing. Now if I do what I do not want to do, it is no longer I who do it, but it is sin living in me that does it.

b.   Defiant Sins or Sins of Rebellion

Sins of rebellion challenge God's authority and sovereignty. In all other unintentional and intentional sins, people do not deny God's goodness and righteousness. In all other sins, people still accept God's kingship and desire to be on God's side. Sins of rebellion are particularly bothersome because here people reject God's leadership.

Smita Valentina

Numbers 14:23 quotes God – *No one who has treated me with contempt will ever see it (Promised Land)*. God had shown Israel numerous miraculous signs and provided for them as He led them out of Egypt. Yet, Israel was constantly unfaithful to God and even challenged God's sovereignty. Of all the adults who left Egypt, only Joshua and Caleb entered the Promised Land. *Exodus-Joshua* foreshadows our own spiritual journey to the Kingdom of God. Our sins of rebellion will deprive us from entering the Kingdom of God, just as the rebel Israelites couldn't enter the Promised Land.

There is no forgiveness for sins of rebellion because the sinner chooses not to repent and be reconciled with God.

The above categorization is a classification of the ways in which we can continue in sin. As we can see, this classification has nothing to do with the scale or magnitude of our sins or their repercussions. Even out of carelessness we can commit very grievous sins with far-reaching effects.

A born-again Christian should not be committing sins in defiance or rebellion. Whenever we are prone to sin or whenever we sin, the Holy Spirit that dwells within us will convict us so that we feel remorse and repent. For a Christian, righteous guilt is normal. In fact, it is healthy and a sign of an awakened conscience. It is a sign that the Holy Spirit is working in us and perfecting us for our heavenly home. If a person claims to be born-again and continues to defy God's authority and holiness, he is a liar.

Born-again Christians are also warned against persisting in ignorance and continuing in unintentional sins. Sin, in the life of a Christian, is a sign of spiritual weakness. If we do not address and remedy our spiritual weakness, we are at high risk of falling back into sin's captivity.

The following steps can help us in living a more responsible life:

A. Examine yourself

Lamentations 3:40 says – *Let us examine our ways and test them, and let us return to the LORD.* A Christian life is a life of introspection. An unexamined life is prone to sin and weaknesses. Even **2 Corinthians 13:5** encourages us to examine ourselves to see whether we are in Christ Jesus. How can we ever know our moral failings if we do reflect upon our own life! And if we are unaware of our weaknesses, how can we even attempt to overcome them!

B. Repent and be reconciled

Our Christian faith is based on grace through faith. **Ephesians 2:8** says – *For it is by grace you have been saved, through faith – and this not from yourselves, it is the gift of God…* This offer of grace does not ever change, so long as we demonstrate faith. Therefore, we always have the guarantee of reconciliation.

1 John 1:9 gives us abundant assurance – *If we confess our sins, he is faithful and just and will forgive us our sins and purify us from all unrighteousness.* But beware, God knows our heart and He examines our motives. **1 John 3:9** says – *No one who is born of God will continue to sin, because God's seed remains in him; he cannot go on sinning, because he has been born of God.*

Further, **Galatians 6:7-8** says – *Do not be deceived: God cannot be mocked. A man reaps what he sows. The one who sows to please his sinful nature, from that nature will reap destruction; the one who sows to please the Spirit, from the Spirit will reap eternal life.* We should be careful not to take God for granted. We shouldn't develop a flippant attitude towards God.

Smita Valentina

C.   Give full control to the Holy Spirit

It is the Holy Spirit that sanctifies us and produces the signs of spiritual maturity in our lives. **Romans 8:9** says – *You, however, are controlled not by the sinful nature but by the Spirit, if the Spirit of God lives in you. And if anyone does not have the Spirit of Christ, he does not belong to Christ.*

We have an obligation towards the Holy Spirit – to give full control of our lives to the Holy Spirit. It is only by the Holy Spirit we can put to death the misdeeds of the body. It is the Holy Spirit that testifies with our spirit that we are God's children. It is the Holy Spirit that helps us in our weakness and intercedes for us. (Ref. **Romans 8**). If we do not let the Holy Spirit work in us and transform us, we grieve the Holy Spirit which is an unforgivable sin. Without the Holy Spirit's presence within us we have no fellowship with God.

D.   Always remember your first love and your position in Christ Jesus

If we want to remain grounded in our faith in Christ Jesus, we must remember 'what we were' and 'what Jesus Christ has done for us'. Without a constant reminder of God's grace in our life, we can easily become conceited. **Ephesians 2** encourages us to remember that once we were separate from God, hopeless; but we were brought near through the blood of Jesus Christ. Apostle Paul often revisited his experience with Jesus Christ.

King David says in **Psalm 51:3** – *my sin is always before me.* After his sin with Bathsheba, King David was cautious to remain humble before God. Our position in Christ Jesus must always be that of grace. It's only when we accept our weakness and humble ourselves before God can we truly experience the power of God's transforming grace.

2 Corinthians 12:9 – *My grace is sufficient for you, for my power is made perfect in weakness.*

Toxic Guilt

Guilt can also be brought about by the schemes of the Devil. This is the **toxic guilt** or **worldly sorrow**. This is the type of guilt that doesn't allow you to let go of your past sins. The Devil attempts to sow seeds of doubt in your heart. The Devil lies to you about how there is no hope for you and you are condemned forever.

I have observed this toxic guilt in Christians especially when they are going through a difficult time. When facing sickness or misfortune, many tend to believe that God is punishing them. We live in an imperfect world. Sickness and sufferings are a part of life. But the Devil will use these normal events in our day to day life to tempt us back into sin.

The Devil will even use people we know to maliciously talk about us and condemn us whenever we are going through difficult times. People will begin judging us harshly for our past. Recall the Book of Job. When God allowed the Devil to test Job, God Himself said – *Have you considered my servant Job? There is no one on earth like him; he is blameless and upright, a man who fears God and shuns evil.* When calamity came upon Job, his friends gathered around him in a great show of sympathy and began accusing him. Eliphaz said in **Job 5:17** – *Blessed is the man whom God corrects; so do not despise the discipline of the Almighty.*

Even though Eliphaz's general argument was valid, it did not apply to Job. Job must have indeed lived a very conscientious life because he was not swayed by the accusations of his friends nor did he let his own reasoning condemn him. Job accepted his suffering and bemoaned it;

but he rejected it as a punishment. I really envy Job's confidence.

The Devil uses toxic guilt by constantly reminding us of our failures. This is a trap essentially for those who set unrealistic standards for themselves. I have found that when I set a very rigid and tight schedule for myself, I fail more systematically. Each day that I fail to follow my schedule to the tiniest detail I tend to antagonize myself. If I don't achieve my unrealistic target, I condemn myself and then waste the next few days just trying to pick myself up. But when I just let myself enjoy my work by setting a very flexible schedule and a lenient target, I realize I achieve much more. Overcoming toxic guilt due to unrealistic standards is one of the toughest challenges. After all, when you take an extra hour nap in the afternoon and the Devil throws verses from Proverbs (such as, **Proverbs 26:14** – *As a door turns on its hinges, so a sluggard turns on his bed*) at you, you may easily start feeling guilty. Is this guilt rational? God does not want us to be lazy and unfruitful; but He also does not want us to over-burden ourselves and experience burn-out.

Chronic toxic guilt is fatal to our faith and it can easily make us backslide. To overcome toxic guilt we must develop spiritual discipline and grow in our personal relationship with God. Remember God's precious promises that God has given to all those believe in Jesus Christ that He has forgiven all our sins and freed us from the captivity of sin. Only by inclining our ears to the voice of God can we silence the voice of the evil one.

SPIRITUAL WEAKNESS

Continuing in sin or our inability to overcome the various kinds of unintentional sins is a result as well as a sign of our spiritual weakness.

What exactly is spiritual weakness?

While we are on this earth, even though we may be born again, we still struggle with the weaknesses of our earthly human nature. The Bible refers to this as the 'sinful nature'. As we grow in our faith, we are called to shed this nature of the flesh and be conformed to the likeness of Jesus Christ.

Romans 8:1-4 gives a beautiful explanation:

Therefore, there is now no condemnation for those who are in Christ Jesus, because through Christ Jesus the law of the Spirit of life set me free from the law of sin and death. For what the law was powerless to do in that it was weakened by the sinful nature, God did by sending his own Son in the likeness of sinful man to be a sin offering. And so he condemned sin in sinful man, in order that the righteous requirements of the law might be fully met in us, who do not live according to the sinful nature but according to the Spirit.

Speaking further of the difference between a sinful fallen person and born-again person, **Romans 8:5-8** says:

Those who live according to the sinful nature have their minds set on what that nature desires; but those who live in accordance with the Spirit have their minds set on what the Spirit desires. The mind of the sinful man is death, but the mind controlled by the Spirit is life and peace; the sinful mind is hostile to God. It does not submit to God's law, nor can it do so. Those controlled by the sinful nature cannot please God.

Christians are called to be led by the Spirit and no longer conform to the pattern of the world – *Do not conform any longer to the pattern of this world, but be transformed by the renewing of your mind. Then you will be able to test and approve what God's will is – his good, pleasing and perfect will.* **(Romans 12:2)**

Smita Valentina

Let me illustrate it in the form of a continuum:

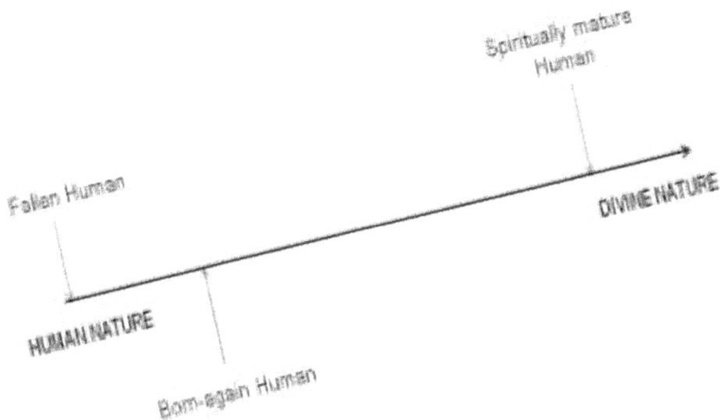

The Bible tells us that we are born sinners because of our sinful nature. **Psalm 51:5** says – *Surely I was sinful at birth, sinful from the time my mother conceived me.* **Ephesians 2:1-3** reiterates this when it says we are born spiritually dead – *As for you, you were dead in your transgressions and sins, in which you used to live when you followed the ways of this world and of the ruler of the kingdom of the air, the spirit who is now at work in those who are disobedient. All of us also lived among them at one time, gratifying the carvings of our sinful nature and following its desires and thoughts. Like the rest, we were by nature objects of wrath.*

Every inclination of humans is towards evil. We notice it in our lives as well when even little children begin demonstrating this sinful nature in their proclivity to learn evil ways – lying, stealing candy, etc. Without the knowledge of God's saving grace through Jesus Christ, people remain in their fallen human nature.

By accepting God's offer of salvation through Jesus Christ, we are born-again – born of the Spirit. God in His immense compassion forgives our sins and endows us with the Holy Spirit to be our Counsellor. As long as we are on this sin-affected world, a born-again person still retains his earthly sinful nature but through the power of the Holy Spirit he is also made able to partake in God's divine nature.

2 Peter 1:3-4 says – *His divine power has given us everything we need for life and godliness through our knowledge of him who called us by his own glory and goodness. Through these he has given us his very great and precious promises, so that through them you may participate in the divine nature and escape the corruption in the world caused by evil desires.* As we give full authority and control of our lives to the Holy Spirit and let the Holy Spirit transform us, gradually we cease being controlled by our sinful desires and are instead led by the Holy Spirit.

Therefore, a spiritual person is not an other-worldly person but a common human being who is led by the Holy Spirit. When a person is born-again, as an infant believer in Christ Jesus he may be more prone to fall into the temptations of the flesh. This doesn't mean that he is not born-again or the Holy Spirit doesn't dwell within him. It simply means that he is still spiritually weak or a spiritual infant. Bible exhorts us to become spiritually mature and demonstrate the fruit of the Holy Spirit in our lives. A born-again Christian must continually move forward towards the divine nature. A born-again Christian may backslide when he/she reverses his/her direction of movement and starts sliding back towards the sinful human nature into his/her old fallen state.

Spiritual growth and maturity is essential in the life of a Christian. Some of the elements of spiritual growth as mentioned in **2 Peter 1:5-9** are:

- Faith in Jesus Christ
- Goodness
- Knowledge of God through the Scriptures
- Self-control
- Perseverance

Smita Valentina

- Godliness
- Brotherly kindness
- Love

Spiritual growth enables us to discern two things:

It is the proof that a person is Born-again

2 Peter 1:10 says – *Therefore, my brothers, be all the more eager to make your calling and election sure. For if you do these things, you will never fall…* **'these things'** refer to the elements of spiritual growth and maturity mentioned in **2 Peter 1:5-9**.

While it is quite natural for a spiritual-infant to have lapses now and then; when a person refuses to mature spiritually it is a sign that the person may not have accepted Christ Jesus as his personal Saviour, Lord and God in the first place. **1 John 3:6** says – *No one who lives in him (i.e. Christ Jesus) keeps on sinning. No one who continues to sin has either seen him or known him.*

Being born-again is not a church mandated activity that everyone must do when they turn 16 or 18. Being born-again is a conviction, a commitment and a choice. It is a conscious choice to give our life to Jesus Christ. By accepting Jesus as our personal Saviour, we commit to say *'NO to all ungodliness'* and God empowers us in doing so by giving us His Spirit. A born-again person must desire to please God and grow in God's grace. (Ref. **Titus 2:11-14**)

It prevents us from continuing in sin

By continually growing towards spiritual maturity, we subdue our sinful human nature, thus preventing moral lapses. Bible encourages us to train ourselves to overcome the world and grow in our likeness of Christ Jesus.

2 Peter 1:5-7 tells us of the elements of spiritual maturity and exhorts us to grow in these qualities. **2 Peter 1:4** precedes these qualities – ... *through them you may participate in the divine nature and escape the corruption in the world caused by evil desires.* Yes, as we increase in our participation in the divine nature, we grow towards holiness. **2 Peter 1:8** sums this – *For if you possess these qualities in increasing measure, they will keep you from being ineffective and unproductive in your knowledge of our Lord Jesus Christ.*

Hebrew 5:13-14 encourages us to grow from infancy towards spiritual maturity – *Anyone who lives on milk, being still an infant, is not acquainted with the teaching about righteousness. But solid food is for the mature, who by constant use have trained themselves to distinguish good from evil.*

How do we identify our spiritual weakness?

Just as it is difficult for us to discern false teachers and false teachings casually, it is quite easy to be unaware of our own spiritual weakness if we do not take time to reflect upon our life. **2 Corinthians 11:13-15** tells us – *For such men are false apostles, deceitful workmen, masquerading as apostles of Christ. And no wonder, for Satan himself masquerades as an angel of light. It is not surprising, then, if his servants masquerades as servants of righteousness.*

If we do not constantly examine our allegiance, we won't even realize when we start furthering Devil's agenda instead of working for the Kingdom of God. Therefore, **2 Corinthians 13:5** tells us – *Examine yourselves to see whether you are in the faith; test yourselves. Do you not realize that Christ Jesus is in you – unless, of course, you fail the test?*

There are quite a few tell-tale signs of spiritual weakness. As we discuss these signs, let us not be weary for **2 Corinthians 10:4-5** tells us – *The weapons we fight with are not the weapons of the world. On the contrary, they have divine power* *to demolish strongholds. We demolish arguments and every pretension that sets itself up against the knowledge of God, and we take captive every thought to make it obedient to Christ.* Let us use this guide to introspect upon our own lives so that we can be better equipped to overcome our spiritual-weaknesses. As we regularly commit our life to God, the Holy Spirit will continue to complete the work of salvation in our lives.

i.　　Lack of Spiritual Growth

One of the first signs of spiritual weakness is lack of spiritual growth. **1 Corinthians 3:1-3** says – *Brothers, I could not address you as spiritual but as worldly – mere infants in Christ. I gave you milk, not solid food, for you were not yet ready for it. Indeed, you are still not ready. You are still worldly. For since there is jealousy and quarrelling among you, are you not worldly.*

Shortly after accepting Jesus in our lives, we may show quick improvement in our spiritual life. However, slowly the fervour cools down and we may stagnate or start backsliding. Most born-again Christians find a sweet spot in the continuum discussed earlier and remain stagnated there. It is quite easy to fall back from that sweet spot.

As a spiritual infant we must crave spiritual milk so that we may grow up in our salvation (Ref. **1 Peter 2:2**); but we must be weaned off milk and progress to solid food so that we grow in grace and knowledge of our Lord and Saviour Jesus Christ and be firm in our faith. (Ref. **2 Peter 3:17-18**)

Hebrews 6 refers to the elementary truths of our Christian faith as milk teachings. These elementary teachings are:

- Repentance from acts that lead to death
- Faith in God
- Instruction about baptism
- Laying on of hands

- Resurrection of the dead
- Eternal judgement

From these elementary teachings, we need to mature towards discernment and reflecting Christ-like character to build the body of Christ on earth. From being fed, we need to reach the state of being able to feed others. Feeding does not only have to do with preaching and teaching. As mature Christians, we need to grow into helping others in their faith, extending and strengthening the Kingdom of God on earth, peace-making and much more.

Ephesians 4:1-2 says – *As a prisoner for the Lord, then, I urge you to live a life worthy of the calling you have received. Be completely humble and gentle; be patient, bearing with one another in love.*

Further, **Ephesians 4:11-16** says – *It was he (i.e. Christ Jesus) who gave some to be apostles, some to be prophets, some to be evangelists, and some to be pastors and teachers, to prepare God's people for works of service, so that the body of Christ may be built up until we reach unity in the faith and in the knowledge of the Son of God and become mature, attaining to the whole measure of the fullness of Christ. Then we will no longer be infants, tossed back and forth by the waves, and blown here and there by every wind of teaching and by the cunning and craftiness of men in their deceitful scheming. Instead speaking the truth in love, we will in all things grow up into him who is the Head, that is, Christ. From him the whole body, joined and held together by every supporting ligament, grows and builds itself up in love, as each part does its work.*

If we find ourselves struggling with the foundational truths of our Christian faith and unable to exercise our faith into everyday acts of righteousness, we might be struggling with spiritual weakness. If we are unable to practice humility, gentleness, patience and forbearing love, we are not growing. If we are struggling to participate in God's works of service for building up the body of Christ, we are still infants.

Smita Valentina

ii.　　　An undisciplined personal prayer life

The craving for spiritual food is essential for a Christian. And, just like an infant always seeks his mother and finds comfort in her bosom; a Christian must have a yearning to commune with his Creator. The absence of desire to spend personal time with God is a sign of our spiritual weakness.

Psalm 42:1-2 sums the desire for personal time with God:

As the deer pants for streams of water, so my soul pants for you, O God. My soul thirsts for God, for the living God. When can I go and meet with God?

I remember the time I accepted Jesus as my personal Saviour, Lord and God. O' how I waited for free time when I would retreat into my secret solitary place and talk to God. I spent every free waking hour at the feet of God praying and meditating on the Word of God. With time, life got busier or so I reasoned as the time I spent with God started reducing. I remember, eventually, there were times when I would go without opening my Bible for days and my only prayer would be the memorised 'Lord's prayer'. Of and on, I would feel the unrest in my heart and return to God. I realized that the days I don't spend time with God in personal prayer and meditation are most challenging. Those are the days I am most vulnerable to temptations.

At times, we may think that it is okay to skip personal prayer and meditation if we attended Church Service or some group Bible Study. Be very alert of such thoughts. Jesus says in **John 15:5-6** – *"I am the vine; you are the branches. If a man remains in me and I in him, he will bear much fruit; apart from me you can do nothing. If anyone does not remain in me, he is like a branch that is thrown away and withers; such branches are picked up, thrown into the fire and burned."* As a parasitic climber may wrap itself around a fruitful vine for support and at times nutrition, many a times we might be rooted somewhere else but cling to a Christian community for some personal reasons or benefits. The church should be very wary of such parasitic climbers because if there are too many of them and they show no desire to be grafted, they can smother the fruitful vine.

Our relationship with the church is a reflection of our personal relationship with Christ Jesus. There is no substitute for personal prayer and meditation. If we get in the habit of neglecting our relationship with Christ Jesus we will not only become unproductive but we are also in the danger of withering away and be eternally destroyed.

iii.   A disorderly and unmanageable schedule

Any schedule that makes you neglect your personal prayer life or compromise on the quality of the works assigned to you is an effective weapon in Devil's arsenal to distract you from your spiritual race. An inability to maintain a healthy and balanced schedule is a sign of spiritual weakness. It reflects upon our everyday life and presents a bad testimony.

I love baking, so I am aware of the costs involved in making cakes and cookies. While the big fancy bakeries tend to overcharge, the small dingy ones give super competitive prices. Trusting the quality of both kinds of establishment is a matter of great risk these days. But when a bakery sells me mini butter cakes at just ten rupees a piece, I instinctively know that the price is too good to be true.

The mini butter cake looks delightful. It has a rich golden brown colour and a mouth-watering buttery aroma. But something is not right. To the uninitiated it may be delightful but to the connoisseur it spells 'spurious'. The colour is not the result of perfect baking but artificial food colour. The butter cake's texture is the result of hydrogenated vegetable oil. The real butter is just brushed over the warm cake.

Smita Valentina

At times we can busy ourselves to the point where we stop thinking. Our relationship with God is based on our position in Christ Jesus – sitting at God's feet. It is this position that enables us to walk steadily in our Christian faith and stand firm against the challenges of the evil one.

Doing too much shifts our focus from God to people. Many believers struggle with saying 'NO', when it comes to church activities or Christian organizations. Soon, they find themselves hopping from one meeting to another or one program to another. They take on responsibilities in far too many organizations or committees than they can manage. As a result, they are struggling themselves and hampering the growth of the church as well.

While over-engagement burns us out and cuts into our own spiritual growth; under-engagement with the body of Christ also hampers our spiritual development. As we saw earlier, spiritual growth requires meaningful engagement with the body of Christ. We may be spending much time in personal prayer and meditation but if we are unable to translate the knowledge we receive from God for building up the body of Christ, we are failing in our duty towards the family of God. That too is a sign of spiritual weakness.

Different people have different capacities and we must understand our own abilities. Here is a simple guide to set an orderly schedule: *Our schedule should not make us neglect our quality personal time with God. It should not cut into our quality family time. Married people need to spend quality time with one another on a daily basis (except for unavoidable circumstances). Similarly, parents must spend quality time with their children – guiding them in their physical and spiritual growth. Family time must also include family prayer. Our schedule should not make us compromise our regular work. It shouldn't make the students skip classes or cut into their study time. It shouldn't make office-goers neglect the quality of their work.*

Colossians 3:23-24 tells us that in everything we are serving Jesus Christ. *We must also make time to regularly be a part of a community of believers. Apart from these, we may take up activities and positions as long as we can give quality time and effort for each of them.* There's no merit or spiritual profit in simply taking up responsibilities and positions without discharging our duties faithfully.

iv.   Loss of joy and hope

Another sign of spiritual weakness is loss of joy in our life. Bible tells us that the joy of the Lord is our strength. When we have an overloaded schedule we suffer burn out. We start neglecting our time with God because *'we are too busy'*. When we make our schedule we allocate the least amount of time to God out of whatever *leftover* time we have because we turn people pleasers. However, it is difficult to please people, many of whom are also facing the same struggles as us. We begin having great expectations from people because we feel we are investing so much time for them. When our expectations are not met we get upset. We have far too many disagreements, and tempers flare. Soon we realize that we are simply doing stuff to maintain appearances. Serving the Lord no longer gives us joy because we do not even feel that we are serving the Lord. This brings guilt and further eats away at our hope when we start questioning our salvation. The farther we stray from God, the easier it is for the Devil to attack us.

v.   Lack of love

Jesus tells us in **Matthew 24:12** – *Because of the increase of wickedness, the love of most will grow cold, but he who stands firm to the end will be saved.* **Revelations 2:4** tells us – *Yet I hold this against you: You have forsaken your first love.*

Smita Valentina

Lack of love in our actions and our relationships is a sure sign of spiritual weakness and spiritual decline. It is our Christ-like love that is our Christian identity. God alone is the source of this Christ-like love. **1 John 4:7** tells us – *love comes from God.* Our neglect of our personal time with God can cost us dearly because it cuts us off from the source of love. Like the Church of Ephesus mentioned in **Revelations 2:1-7**, we may be excelling in good deeds, working hard and persevering without growing weary; but without love it all amounts to nothing. Where there is no love there is no God.

vi.   Ineffective ministry

Spiritual weakness can affect anyone if we are not watchful. It is more dangerous for congregations when church leaders suffer from spiritual weaknesses. When our walk and talk do not match, it's a serious issue. People do not just listen to our words and sermons; they are closely watching our lives as well. The dissonance between our everyday living and church appearance causes our ministry to be ineffective.

Ineffective ministry can be recognized easily when there is a serious dearth in second line leadership. God-centric ministry ensures that we prepare others to take leadership positions. **2 Timothy 2:2** says – *And the things you have heard me say in the presence of many witnesses entrust to reliable men who will also be qualified to teach others.* In a godman-centric ministry, the leader finds it difficult to delegate and share power or control. There's also constant clash amongst church leaders which often leads to congregations breaking up.

There's also another form of ministry which is in vogue today – people-centric ministry. It draws heavily from marketing strategies taught in business schools. People-centric ministries focus on activities according to the likes and preferences of the congregants. These ministries have come up just as **2 Timothy 4:3-4** forewarned:

For the time will come when men will not put up with sound doctrine. Instead, to suit their own desires, they will gather around them a great number of teachers to say what their itching ears want to hear. They will turn their ears away from the truth and turn aside to myths.

Ineffective ministry effects church growth both numerically and spiritually. We may be trying multiple methods of outreach but we don't see commensurate results. When people do not experience God's love and joy in a congregation they may not associate with it for a long time. At the same time when faithful believers see the priorities of their church shifting, they may choose to abandon ship.

Personal attention to new members is very crucial in making them feel welcome. New members may require more nurturing and nourishment to grow in their faith. When our schedule is overloaded, we may not be able to give adequate attention such new members which will eventually hamper their spiritual growth.

Therefore, it's important that we evaluate our ministry and interactions to discern our spiritual weakness. It is quite easy for God's *House of Prayer* to turn to a *Den of robbers* if we are not in a God-centric ministry.

vii.   Pride

Another very obvious sign of spiritual weakness is spiritual pride. Jesus has called us to emulate his humility. However, when we start receiving attention even for our spiritual life it is easy to become conceited. Also, knowledge can puff us up if it is just head knowledge and not heart knowledge. (Ref. **1 Corinthians 8:1**)

Smita Valentina

It is very difficult to manage pride. We may display arrogance, at times even thoughtlessly, because of our wealth, our status and position in society, our connections, our appearances, our gifts and talents, etc. Anything that makes us look down on others is a sign of pride.

Many a times, we can be quite insensitive to other's feelings. The idea of a community event or church service is not to show-off ones gifts and abilities but to build a sense of togetherness. Someone may not be a very good singer, but if one wants to glorify God in a song of praise, we must show our appreciation and praise God for that brother or sister. Someone may not be a very good cook but if he/she brings a dish we must accept it with thanksgiving. Humility accepts everyone as they are. Pride tends to reject everyone even for minor shortcomings.

Spiritual pride is the pride one develops based on their spiritual condition. People infected with spiritual pride look down at others for their spiritual weaknesses in judgement. They are always quick to speak because they consider themselves more knowledgeable. They are quick to enter into meaningless arguments and do not give up easily. They are quick to point out other's mistakes.

While we are to admonish and correct others when they err; the difference between spiritual pride and godly wisdom is that pride is always loveless while godly wisdom is compassionate. There is a very thin line between the two and we must be very careful because wisdom is a sign of spiritual maturity and pride is a sign of spiritual weakness (even sin). If we live an unexamined life, we may have the vice of spiritual pride but we may continue to believe that we are displaying godly wisdom.

viii.   Anger

Anger is our natural reaction to many triggers. We may experience anger if we are disappointed with others. A boss wants his/her subordinate to finish an urgent report. If the subordinate fails to perform his/her duty, the boss may get angry. Parents get angry when children are disobedient. Children may get angry with their parents if they are too strict or unreasonable. We may get angry at ourselves if we make careless mistakes. We get angry if somebody abuses us or cheats us. Many a times our anger may be reasonable and justifiable. However, we must remember that our response to anger can lead us to sin. There is a very delicate line between righteous anger and sinful anger.

In the Bible, we often read about God's righteous anger. God was angry with the Israelites and other sinful nations because their ways were evil and they affected the innocent. But, how did God respond to His righteous anger? God demonstrates immense patience while dealing with people. He warns them repeatedly and disciplines them in various ways. That's why **Lamentation** notes – Because of God's great love we are not consumed.

Since anger is a normal emotion, it is not a sin in itself; how we express our anger can be a sin. Let's recall Cain's sin. In his anger, he murdered his own brother, Abel. Anger can make us do harmful things. It can cause 'fits of rage' where we lose all reason and inflict serious damage to others and even ourselves. It can make us curse and even physically assault others. We can use harsh words that can break relationships. Anger can make us envious and vengeful.

Therefore, **James 1:19-20** says – *My dear brothers, take note of this: Everyone should be quick to listen, slow to speak and slow to become angry, for man's anger does not bring about the righteous life that God desires.*

Smita Valentina

ix.   Lack of warmth in repentance and inability to forgive

Our inability to forgive others just as God has forgiven us is also a sign of our spiritual weakness. We may forgive with our words but our actions say otherwise. We hold on to grudges and it becomes evident in our social interactions. If someone has hurt us grievously, it is understandable that a perfect restoration of our broken relationship can be quite challenging. However, forgiveness demands that we do not let our past experience colour our present attitude.

Two gentlemen do not get along very well. Apparently, Mr. Mark had deceived Mr. Paul a long time ago and Mr. Paul lost a lot of money. Now, Mr. Mark has made full restitution for the loss that Mr. Paul had incurred and begged for his forgiveness. Mr. Paul assured Mr. Mark that he has forgiven him completely. Mr. Mark is a changed man now and he is quite gifted. So, when there's a need for a new project director in the church, he applied for the position. Mr. Paul is on the board that approves appointments. Even though all the other board members approve of Mr. Mark as the new project director because he has shown faithfulness over the past ten years, Mr. Paul continues to veto the decision. Do you think Mr. Paul has really forgiven Mr. Mark?

Forgiving someone does not necessarily mean that we need to become best friends with those who hurt us but we should not continue to punish our offenders in subtle ways. Rather, as Christians, we must rejoice as we witness growth and maturity in our past offenders.

Since we continue holding grudge against those who have hurt us; we imagine the same with those whom we have hurt which takes away the warmth of being forgiven. We keep assuming that no one can forgive us completely and they will never be on our side. We do not turn to them in times of need and we fail to fulfil our Christian duty towards others.

x.   Failure to give priority to God

Spiritual growth and maturity enables us to understand God's holiness. When we are not growing spiritually, we fail to grasp God's greatness. We begin taking God's works for granted. If the Prime Minister of our country comes to address an office meeting, we won't arrive casually twenty minutes late. Forget the Prime Minister; even if our office boss calls a meeting at 8:00 am in the morning, we will arrive punctually. If an exam starts at 10:00 am, the students will be seated in the examination hall by 9:45 am. Then, why do we fail to keep our appointments and engagements involving God's work.

Many a times, people arrive at an important church or Christian organization meeting unprepared. We keep forgetting deadlines and our own responsibilities. Sometimes, we even forget to prepare for a Bible study, even though we would be the one leading it. Our focus reflects our priorities. We may frequently say that we must give first priority to God but our flippant attitude towards God is reflected in the way we appear before God.

Our earthly duties are no doubt essential. I am not talking about rescheduling your office appointments to suit your church obligations. Rather, I am taking about the everyday small things that we ourselves plan but fail to honour. For example: If we commit to lead a Bible Study on a particular date and time, most certainly we give our commitment because our schedule was open for that slot. So, if we forget about it and fill that slot with something else, it can mean either of the two things: God and God's work isn't our priority or we lead a very undisciplined life.

If we are not showing signs of spiritual growth, it is time to re-evaluate our priorities and commitment to God.

Smita Valentina

SPIRITUAL DISCIPLINE

Christians are born of the Spirit and called to be led by the Holy Spirit. Being born again, though we retain our mortal human nature as long as we are on this earth; we have a higher calling to join in the spiritual or divine nature of God.

When we are newly born-again, we are spiritual infants. Gradually, we must grow in our spiritual maturity. This growth is brought about by the sanctifying work of Holy Spirit who dwells in us. However, as free-willed human beings we need to constantly bring ourselves to total submission before Holy Spirit for the accomplishment of a transformed life.

This is where "Spiritual Discipline" is of paramount significance. Spiritual Discipline is about disciplining ourselves to submit to Holy Spirit.

Theologians have attempted to classify and list a number of ways in which we can build "Spiritual Discipline" in our lives. They call it – *Spiritual Disciplines*. These disciplines enable us to place our minds, bodies and our temperaments before the transformative power of the Holy Spirit and seek God's grace to grow in His image and likeness. These Spiritual Disciplines not only transform us inwardly but they enable us to be faithful witnesses for Christ Jesus in our thoughts, words and actions.

Two of the most popular categorizations of "Spiritual Disciplines" come from *Richard J. Foster* and *Dallas Willard*:

Richard J. Foster, in his book *Celebration of Discipline,* developed a three-fold categorization –

- **Inward disciplines** – Meditation, Prayer, Fasting and Study
- **Outward disciplines** – Simplicity, Solitude, Submission and Service

- **Corporate disciplines** – Confession, Worship, Guidance and Celebration

Dallas Willard, in *Spirit of the Disciplines*, categorized the spiritual disciplines into two classes –

- **Disciplines of Abstinence** – Solitude, Silence, Fasting, Frugality, Chastity, Secrecy and Sacrifice
- **Disciplines of Engagement** – Study, Worship, Celebration, Service, Prayer, Fellowship, Confession and Submission

Based on the above mentioned categorizations and my personal meditations on the Word of God through the guidance of Holy Spirit, I have found the following practices to be most practical and effective. I prefer calling them 'habits' that enable us to grow in our spiritual discipline:

A. HABITS THAT BUILD OUR RELATIONSHIP WITH GOD

It is presumptuous of us to even think that once we are born-again in Christ Jesus and receive the Holy Spirit through faith in Jesus, it is totally up to the Holy Spirit to work in us. Holy Spirit is not like a genie that grants our whims. Holy Spirit is the third-person of the triune God-head and equally important as the Father and the Son. It is the Holy Spirit that makes witnessing and holy living possible. In fact, we witness the continued presence and powerful manifestation of the Holy Spirit throughout the Bible right from creation to the Book of Revelation. Unfortunately, we fail to witness the power of the Holy Spirit in our lives because we fail to acknowledge and revere Him. Often, we fail to manifest the fruit of the Spirit and grow in spiritual maturity because we do not submit ourselves before God, the Holy Spirit.

Our relationship with God is built on God's love and grace. However, our spiritual growth in this relationship is based on – how we reciprocate God's love through humble submission, obedience and reverential fear. We grow and become fruitful in our relationship with God by cultivating the following habits:

- **Meditating on the Word of God**

There is much difference between reading, studying and meditation. We can read the Bible simply like browsing a magazine or reading a thrilling novel. We may remember it like a fascinating epic but mere reading may not help us know God more intimately. Many people study the Bible as an academic exercise. The Bible is the most widely studied compendium. It is extensively researched from different perspectives – archaeological, cultural, linguistics, religious studies, semiotics, etc. These studies may further the understanding of cultural and religious evolution but it may not necessarily enable us to draw nearer to God. What makes *'meditation'* on the Word of God so special is that it is led by the Holy Spirit. We cannot grow in spiritual discipline without the Holy Spirit and the continuous working of the Holy Spirit in our lives. The Word of God is inspired by the Holy Spirit and it can only be revealed to us through the Holy Spirit.

Therefore, we must cultivate the habit of mediating on the Word of God frequently to develop spiritual discipline. At times, it may feel difficult because we are weak-willed human beings, but as we devote our time regularly in coming before God we will eventually overcome our spiritual weakness.

- **Prayer and Fasting**

Jesus emphasised on the essentiality of prayer and fasting in Christian life. One of the most important works of prayer in our lives is to enable us to overcome temptations. Prayer is our communion with God. We pour our hearts out to God in prayer and wait upon the Lord for His response. In prayer, we sit before God in humble submission and let Him reveal His will and His plan and purpose for us. We may also simply sit in silent prayer before God and let His search our hearts and comfort us. We come before God in prayer because we want to know Him more and draw nearer to Him.

We can pray without fasting but we cannot fast without prayer. Fasting without prayer is meaningless. Fasting has spiritual merit when we become aware of what it is meant to achieve. There are times when I forget to eat if I am too engrossed in some work. Can I call it fasting? I know of many young people who get so busy in their office that, coupled with an undisciplined life, they have their first bite of food well after 2 or 3 p.m. in the afternoon. Can we call that fasting? Fasting is not mere denial of food – it is denial of the self, so that the power of the Holy Spirit can take over us. It has to be conscious. It must be free from other worldly distractions as well. It must include prayer.

Denying oneself on a regular basis enables us to overcome the weaknesses of the flesh and grow in our spiritual strength.

- **Solitude**

We find it easier to study the Word of God in a group and have a time of fasting and prayer with our community of believers; but to grow in our relationship with God we need to spend quality personal time with God. Jesus often sought solitude to connect with the Father (ref. **Luke 5:16**). If Jesus retreated to solitary places so often, imagine how much solitude we need to make our relationship with God fruitful. This personal one-on-one time with God is so vital because it enables us to commune directly with God. Now we have direct access to God through Jesus Christ; it's unfortunate that many of us continue to approach God indirectly. God wants to have one-on-one relationship with us. We are not distantly related to God. We must remember that we are God's children and He removed all barriers that separated us so that we can have a living relationship.

- **Silence**

Silence, like solitude, is something most of us are a bit uncomfortable with. Most of us are not used to silence and it can be quite overwhelming. I have always been a loner. I have my moments of being very social; but about 80% of the time, I prefer my solitude. Still, when I accepted Christ and came before God in silence, I was overwhelmed by the noises in my head. Even those who enjoy solitude may not always enjoy silence. Many of us may put on music or recorded gospel messages to drown the silence.

Silence is powerful. It is during this time of silence that we hear God's still small voice like a tiny whisper. It is during this time of silence that the Holy Spirit revealed to me my weaknesses and my hidden faults and made it easier for me to confess before God and grow in my knowledge of God. Over time, this silence has become a cherished time when I experience the unalloyed joy of fellowship with the Holy Spirit.

Our personal prayers are often quite wordy. We have grown up with the culture of lengthy prayers. While in a public setting, prayers are also meant to encourage and edify the congregation; personal prayers are between us and God, and God does not need our encouragement or edification. **Habakkuk 2:20** says – *But the LORD is in his holy temple; let all the earth be silent before him.* Sometimes, let God do the talking!!!

Jesus also taught about prayer in **Matthew 6:5-15**. Our prayers shouldn't always be a list of demands from God because our heavenly Father knows what we need. Instead, our silence before God should enable us to discern what God wants from us.

Ecclesiastes 5:1-3 speaks of virtue of silence:

Guard your steps when you go to the house of God. Go near to listen rather than to offer the sacrifice of fools, who do not know that they do wrong. Do not be quick with your mouth, do not be hasty in your heart to utter anything before God. God is in heaven and you are on earth, so let your words be few. As a dream comes when there are many cares, so the speech of a fool when there are many words.

B. HABITS THAT BUILD OUR RELATIONSHIP WITH THE FAMILY OF GOD

The greatest commandment asks us to *love God and love one another*. When we love God we manifest God's love by loving the family of God. Our love for God's family is expressed by our desire to engage with one another in various meaningful ways. The gifts and fruit of the Holy Spirit is to be shared with others. **1 Corinthians 12:7** says – *Now to each one the manifestation of the Spirit is given for the common good.* By engaging with the body of Christ i.e. the Church, we use our spiritual gifts for the building and strengthening of the Church.

- **Corporate Worship**

One of the essential habits to build our relationship with God's family on earth is by worshipping together. Christians who have a strong relationship with God cannot go without corporate worship i.e. worshipping with other like-minded believers. We must connect with a body of believers to grow in our spiritual discipline and life. We cannot fulfil the second part of the greatest command – *love one another* – without *'another'*. Worshipping together is one of the ways in which we celebrate God's love and faithfulness. By worshipping together we express the joy and hope we have in Christ Jesus our Lord. Corporate worship should not turn into a 'one-man-show'. It should be orderly and enable everyone to use their spiritual gifts to glorify God and edify the congregation in turns (Ref. **1 Corinthians 14:26-33**). Everything should be done in a fitting and orderly way for the strengthening of the church.

Our Christian journey is quite long and it requires immense patience and perseverance to complete the race marked out for us. The joy that emanates from corporate worship can be instrumental in keeping our spiritual fervour alive. Therefore, as **Hebrews 10:24-25** notes – *Let us consider how we may spur one another on towards love and good deeds. Let us not give up meeting together, as some are in the habit of doing, but let us encourage one another – and all the more as you see the Day approaching.*

- **Fellowship**

We must also inculcate the habit of fellowship with the children of God. Fellowship and corporate worship are not one and the same. Fellowship may incorporate the element of corporate worship; but it is much more than that. I prefer small congregations because it gives ample time and opportunity to know each member personally. In many large congregations, people attend a Church Service and disperse without even meeting and greeting anyone. Today, many congregations are competing against one another. They want to show that they have the largest number of congregants or the biggest church building. I am of the opinion that if a church building becomes too small for the congregation, it is better to build another one instead of a larger one. A large congregation of thousands of congregants is non-conducive to meaningful fellowship. Most of the congregants will never get an opportunity to share their spiritual gifts or participate in leadership positions in such large congregations. Most members may never get an opportunity to even know the other members of the church. Though the numbers may be quite impressive, such congregations have a large number of spiritual infants who never grow into maturity.

Fellowship involves sharing and caring for one another. In fellowship, we engage with one another in personal ways through – guidance and counselling, teaching and training, correction, etc. It is through fellowship that we understand the unique spiritual and physical needs of individuals and support one another in brotherly love and kindness.

Fellowship can be church-led, such as cottage prayer meetings, special retreats and programmes, picnics, etc. It can also be individual-initiated. We must try to visit our fellow brothers and sisters in Christ Jesus, not only in times of need, but also as our expression of love. However, we must also exercise caution that we do not make others weary with our frequent visits (ref. **Proverbs 25:17**). Take small gifts along. Keep the visits short. And always, pray for the family you visit.

Another element of fellowship is helping one another in times of need. We must always try to offer our time, our resources and our efforts to our fellow brothers and sisters in Christ Jesus when they are in need. But when we are in need, we must also be careful to not take undue advantage of our fellow believer's generosity and kindness and over-burden them.

Smita Valentina

- **Christian Giving**

Christian giving is a gift of grace. It is essential to our spiritual growth and full participation in our fellowship with God. **2 Corinthians 8:7** encourages us to excel in giving – *But just as you excel in everything – in faith, in speech, in knowledge, in complete earnestness and in your love for us – see that you also excel in this grace of giving.*

Frankly speaking, tithing is biblical but not necessarily Christian. However, the modern-day churches continue to teach about tithing probably because most Christians are very poor in Christian giving. Today, most churches take on big projects that require a lot of money; and if the spiritually-infant congregants were not threatened with curses for their failure to tithe regularly, the projects will never see the light of day. Personally, I don't approve of this method to make people give because it is not Christian.

In the Old Testament, Abraham gave a tenth of everything to Melchizedek. God did not command Abraham to tithe. It was Abraham's free-will offering. Later, Jacob promised a tenth of everything to God at Bethel. Even here, God did not ask Jacob for anything. It was Jacob's vow.

Tithing was formally established in the Book of Leviticus. Its purpose was to support the Levites as they ministered before the LORD. The Levites were not granted land for agricultural and pastoral purpose. God was their portion. A portion of the tithe also went for the regular maintenance of the Tabernacle.

Today, there is no Levitical priesthood to require a tenth of everything for their sustenance; nor do we have an elaborate ceremonial mandate to fulfill. So, we must move from mere tithing to Christian Giving.

Christian Giving should not be limited to tithing or Sunday offerings. If we understand the essence of *'giving that God requires of us'*, we will develop a healthy attitude towards Christian Giving.

Christian Giving should be an act of faith that God is our provider; and an act of gratitude for all that God has done for us. The Israelites were not required to bring their tithes before the harvest. They were to bring their tithes after the harvest i.e. after experiencing God's faithfulness in blessing them with bounty. They gave in line with the blessings they had received. Christian Giving is an expression of God's blessings in our life.

We must also give willingly to support God's work on earth. Though the Levitical priesthood is abolished, today we have people who give their full-time to serve God and God's children. We have full-time missionaries, pastors, teachers and other church-workers who must be given regular salaries (Ref. **1 Timothy 5:18**). We also have physical assets like church buildings and grounds that require maintenance. We need resources to reach out to the unreached and support fellow believers in need.

The new requirements of Christian Giving requires that we give generously and cheerfully (**2 Corinthians 9:6-7**); sacrificially (**Luke 21:1-4**); and compassionately (**James 2:15-16**).

Furthermore, Christian Giving must be in secret (**Matthew 6:1-4**). Yes, financial transactions require to be accounted for so that they are not misappropriated. If we give to any organization, we must ask for a receipt. However, they shouldn't be advertised. In this digital age, we have become prone to advertising our 'giving' as well as 'good works'. Christian Giving requires that the giver glorifies God and the beneficiary is not humiliated. Right Christian Giving develops compassion, gratitude and humility.

Smita Valentina

- **Good Works**

Ephesians 2:10 says – *For we are God's workmanship, created in Christ Jesus to do good works, which God prepared in advance for us to do.* Good works do not grant us salvation but they are a reflection of our salvation. **James 2:18** challenges us – *But someone will say, "You have faith; I have deeds." Show me your faith without deeds, and I will show you my faith by what I do.*

Remember, we are not saved by good works but we are saved for good works. God has prepared these 'good works' in advance for us to perform. If we do not do them, they remain undone. Almost all the epistles encourage us to do good works:

Hebrews 13:16 – *And do not forget to do good and to share with others, for with such sacrifices God is pleased.*

Titus 3:8 – *This is a trustworthy saying. And I want you to stress these things, so that those who have trusted in God may be careful to devote themselves to doing what is good. These things are excellent and profitable for everyone.*

Galatians 6:9-10 – *Let us not become weary in doing good, for at the proper time we will reap a harvest if we do not give up. Therefore, as we have opportunity, let us do good to all people, especially to those who belong to the family of believers.*

Our good works bring glory to God. No one is going to ask us about our faith it we do not demonstrate it through our actions. Therefore, Jesus says in **Matthew 5:16** – *In the same way, let your light shine before men, that they may see your good deeds and praise your Father in heaven.*

Excelling in good works is essential to spiritual maturity. In the beginning, we may find it difficult to involve ourselves in good works because they are acts of sacrificial love. We need to give our time, our strength, and our resources for doing good works. But we must develop a habit of making use of the opportunities available to us to do good. A lack of good deeds is a sign of spiritual weakness and as **James 4:17** warns – *Anyone, the, who know the good he ought to do and doesn't do it, sins.*

       Let's take time each day to examine our lives so that we can become aware of our spiritual status; and let us continue to develop good Christian habits that can help us build spiritual discipline.

       God is faithful; and I am sure as we surrender ourselves to the working of the Holy Spirit ,we will be able to overcome the burden of sin, guilt and temptations and finish our Christian race victoriously in Jesus Christ our Lord.

****

Smita Valentina

III

FORGIVENESS

Forgiveness

Smita Valentina

III

Forgiveness means peace with God. In the previous sections we have discussed that God's forgiveness is available to all those who seek Him. If we acknowledge our sins before God and repent; God is gracious in forgiving us all our sins.

God's forgiveness, as mentioned in the Bible, is a uniquely beautiful gift. A deeper understanding of God's forgiveness is essential for us because we are called to forgive one another just as God has forgiven us. **Ephesians 4:32** – *Be kind and compassionate to one another, forgiving each other, just as in Christ God forgave you.*

In this section of the book, we are going to discuss the beauty of God's forgiveness. We will see what it means to be forgiven by God and how we can receive this forgiveness in our life. We will see how God's forgiveness transforms us and inspires us to forgive others. Finally, we will also discuss how forgiveness leads us to fruitfulness.

GOD'S GRACIOUS GIFT OF FORGIVENESS

The most devastating effect of sin is that sin separates us from God. Any sin, no matter how big or how small, makes us unholy. When Adam and Eve sinned they were separated from God. Even before they were ousted from the Garden of Eden, they hid from God because in their sinful state they could not stand before God's holiness. Their glory was lost. Their nakedness was exposed.

The penalty for sin is death. By committing sin we become unholy and we must die lest we pollute others around us. If God was merciless, we would all have perished a long time ago for all have sinned and fall short of God's glory. But God, in His infinite mercy, chooses to forgive us. **Lamentations 3:22** is such a great comfort – *Because of the LORD's great love we are not consumed, for his compassions never fail.*

In the Old Testament Mosaic Law, God instituted a way for Israel to be reconciled with Him through sacrificial offerings. These sacrifices were symbolic and they reminded the sinner of the gravity and penalty for sin. These sacrifices were meant to evoke repentance and turn the sinner away from his life of sin.

Let us see what the sacrificial offerings, according to the Mosaic Law, demanded:

When anyone sinned and was made aware of his sin; he was to present a sin offering before the LORD. The kind of animal to be sacrificed as a sin-offering depended on the position of the offender in the society rather than his sin.

- Anointed priest – Young bull
- Leader – Male goat
- Common person – Female goat or lamb
- Poor person – Dove or pigeon
- Very poor person – Tenth of an *ephah* of fine flour

The offerings were meant to drive home invaluable lessons that:

- Sin required sacrifice. It had to cost the offender something. Since the Israelites were a pastoral community, they were to sacrifice an animal without defect. They had to offer an animal that could have fetched them very good price. They couldn't offer a defective animal to God.

Smita Valentina

- The anointed priests and leaders were to be role models for the society so they had to pay a higher price for their sins.
- The opportunity for atonement and reconciliation was available to the poorest of the poor.

The procedure for making the sin offering symbolized the following:

- The offender had to present the animal to be sacrificed at the entrance to the Tent of Meeting before the LORD. It symbolized the offender's desire to be reconciled and return to God.
- The offender had to lay his hand on the head of the sacrificial animal signifying the transfer of guilt.
- Further, he had to slaughter the animal signifying that he was the reason why the innocent animal had to die.

This should have been an impactful role-play if the offenders approached the Tent of Meeting with sincere repentance.

Without self-examination, even meaningful practices can easily turn into mere traditions. It was expected that the guilt and cost associated with the sacrificial offerings would deter people from continuing in sin. However, these institutionalized sacrificial offerings could not take away the sins of the people and bring them nearer to God. Therefore, it is written in **1 Samuel 15:22** –

"Does the LORD delight in burnt offerings and sacrifices as much as in obeying the voice of the LORD? To obey is better than sacrifice, and to heed is better than the fat of rams."

Later **Hosea 6:6** notes (*and this verse was quoted by Jesus Christ multiple times*) – *For I desire mercy, not sacrifice, and acknowledgement of God rather than burnt offerings.*

Israel's ceremonial sacrifices did not please God. It was unacceptable to God because it was ineffective in producing repentance. Therefore, King David mentions in **Psalm 51:16-17,**

You do not delight in sacrifice, or I would bring it; you do not take pleasure in burnt offerings.

The sacrifices of God are a broken spirit; a broken and contrite heart, O God, you will not despise.

One of the most fascinating things about God's forgiveness is that it is God who always takes the first step towards reconciliation. It was God who called out to Adam in the Garden of Eden. It was God who questioned Cain. God sent Prophet Nathan to confront King David. God instituted the law for propitiation or divine retribution through sacrificial offerings. It was God who chose to dwell amongst Israel. God led them out of Egypt. He watched over them, provided for them and fought their battles. And when the Old Law proved ineffective in removing sin and guilt; God made a way for us to be reconciled to Him through His Son Jesus Christ.

Jesus Christ came as the permanent High Priest and the perfect unblemished eternal sacrifice to take upon himself the guilt of the whole world and bring eternal peace to all those who accept his gift of forgiveness. He fulfilled the righteous requirements of the Law and by believing in him and obeying him we can inherit his righteousness.

The book of Hebrews presents to us the transition from the Old Covenant to the New Covenant. **Hebrew 9:11-15** highlights –

When Christ came as the high priest of the good things that are already here, he went through the greater and more perfect tabernacle that is not man-made, that is to say, not a part of this creation. He did not enter by means of the blood of goats and calves; but he entered the Most Holy Place once for all by his own blood, having obtained eternal redemption. The blood of goats and bulls and the ashes of a heifer sprinkled on those who are ceremonially unclean sanctify them so that they are outwardly clean. How much more, then, will the blood of Christ, who through the eternal Spirit offered himself unblemished to God, cleanse our consciences from acts that lead to death, so that we may serve the living God!

For this reason Christ is the mediator of a new covenant, that those who are called may receive the promised eternal inheritance – now that he has died as a ransom to set them free from the sins committed under the first covenant.

The uniqueness of God's gracious gift of forgiveness is based on His unfathomable love for us. **John 3:16** sums it up pretty neatly – *For God so loved the world that he gave his one and only Son, that whoever believes in him shall not perish but have eternal life.*

Jesus illustrated God's redeeming love for us through the *Parable of the Prodigal Son.* (Ref. **Luke 15:11-32**)

In a show of great disrespect and rebellion, the younger son demanded his share of property from his father and broke all ties with him. He took his share of inheritance and set off for a distant land where he squandered away all his inheritance. When there was a famine in that distant land, the lost son, now broke, couldn't even get a respectable job. All he could get was a lowly job of feeding pigs. The pay was so meagre that he even longed to eat pig-feed. It was in this dejected state that he remembered his father. He recalled that even his father's servants had plenty of food to spare. When the realization of his sin in rejecting his father's parenthood dawned on him, he was filled with remorse. He decided to return and seek forgiveness from his father. He acknowledged that he had lost his right to sonship, and he hoped that his father would hire him as a servant.

Now we witness God's grace and love.

The son had disrespected and hurt his father. For his rebellion, the father could have had his son stoned to death in accordance with **Deuteronomy 21:18-21**. Instead, the father was longing for his son's return. While the son was still a long way off, the father saw him and ran to him. Did you notice: It's the father than ran to his son!

The son was returning in a very pathetic state. He would have been filthy from his work at the pig-sty. His father appears not to be bothered by his external appearance. He is filled with compassion for his son. Even before the son has washed himself clean, the father hugs him and kisses him.

The son's return reflected his repentance. He had rehearsed a confession and apology, but the father knew his son's heart even before he could complete his speech. For the father, his son's return was all that mattered. The father did not take any account of his son's past actions. He did not scold him or punish him. He was just overjoyed that his son had returned to him.

Though the prodigal son had already taken his share of inheritance and broken ties with his family; the father had prepared a place in advance for his return. The best robe, the ring, the sandals were ready. The calf had already been fattened. The father was eagerly waiting to reinstate his son to his original position of sonship.

That's the kind of love that God has shown us. **1 John 3:1** notes – *How great is the love the Father has lavished on us that we should be called children of God!*

Our return is all that matters to God. No matter how ugly our sins are; God's love and forgiveness is always available to us if we repent and return to Him. God knows what we are going through. He is aware of our weaknesses and our struggles. Like the prodigal son, we needn't stay in the filth of our sin any longer for there is complete redemption when we return to our heavenly Father.

Psalm 103:8-12 says,

> *The LORD is compassionate and gracious,*
> *slow to anger, abounding in love.*
> *He will not always accuse,*
> *nor will he harbour his anger forever;*
> *he does not treat us as our sins deserve*
> *or repay us according to our iniquities.*
> *For as high as the heavens are above the earth,*
> *so great is his love for those who fear him;*
> *as far as the east is from the west,*
> *so far has he removed our transgressions from us.*

ATTRIBUTES OF GOD'S FORGIVENESS

God's forgiveness is where life truly begins. Many a times, when our understanding of God's forgiveness is not holistic, we can easily be tempted to doubt our salvation which rests on God's forgiveness. This can keep us from achieving confidence in our prayers and our witnessing. The Devil will continue to torment us so that we dwell in our guilt and shame and fail to experience the joy of the Lord. Therefore, it is very important for us to understand all about the gracious forgiveness that comes from God when we return to Him in repentance.

1. **God's forgiveness overflows out of his unfathomable enduring love**

Romans 5:8 notes – *But God demonstrates his own love for us in this: While we were still sinners, Christ died for us.*

God does not forgive us when we prove that we are worth His forgiveness. Repentance does not move God's heart to forgive us, for His gift of forgiveness has been made available to us through Christ Jesus while we were still steeped in sin. Our repentance brings us to a realization of God's enduring love and ever present offer of salvation. It enables us to see our own unworthiness and witness God's abounding grace. It makes us realize our need for God. *Let's recall the parable of the prodigal son* – We do not see the father wait for his younger son to make a full confession and beg for mercy and forgiveness. Instead, the father stands waiting with open arms to receive his son. God does not treat us as our sins deserve but He forgives us according to the riches of His great mercy and love.

2. God's forgiveness is perfect and complete

The perfection of God's forgiveness covers all aspects of freedom from sin. When we return to God, He frees us from the penalty of our sins. Then, God gives us His Holy Spirit that enables us to overcome the power of sin in our life. And finally, God gives us the hope and the promise of eternal life in heaven where there is perfect freedom from the presence of sin. God's forgiveness renews us. **2 Corinthians 5:17** – *Therefore, if anyone is in Christ, he is a new creation; the old has gone, the new has come!*

According to God's promise in **Ezekiel 36:25-27** which says – *"I will sprinkle clean water on you, and you will be clean; I will cleanse you from all your impurities and from all your idols. I will give you a new heart and I will put a new spirit in you; I will remove from you your heart of stone and give you a heart of flesh. And I will put my Spirit in you and move you to follow my decrees and be careful to keep my laws"* – the cleansing blood of Jesus Christ purifies us from all our iniquities and infirmities and the Holy Spirit empowers us to live in obedience to God.

God not only forgives us our sins, He also removes our guilt and shame. **Isaiah 57:16,18** says – *I will not accuse forever,* *nor will I always be angry...I have seen his ways, but I will heal him; I will guide him and restore comfort to him...*

Speaking of the new covenant through Jesus Christ, the LORD says in **Jeremiah 31:34** – *For I will forgive their wickedness and will remember their sins no more.* This is the confidence we have in God's forgiveness that God will never count our sins against us once we confess and repent of our sins.

3.   God's forgiveness is infinite

God's infinite goodness in forgiving us is His enduring quality. From the beginning of creation we have witnessed God's immense patience with us.

Isaiah 1:18 says –

"Come now, let us reason together," says the LORD.
"Though your sins are like scarlet,
they shall be as white as snow;
though they are red as crimson,
they shall be like wool."

When we return to God in repentance, God does not pick and choose what sins He would forgive and what He won't. God is faithful in forgiving us from all our sins no matter how big or small they are. **1 John 1:9** notes – *If we confess our sins, he is faithful and just and will forgive us our sins and purify us from all unrighteousness.*

God does not only forgive all our sins, He removes them far from us. **Psalm 103:12** affirms – *As far as the east is from the west, so far has he removed our transgressions from us.*

Micah 7:19 says – *You will again have compassion on us; you will tread our sins underfoot and hurl all our iniquities into the depths of the sea.*

4.   God delights in forgiving us

The father, in the *parable of the prodigal son*, was so delighted that he celebrated his son's return. Jesus concludes *the parable of the lost sheep* in **Luke 15:7** – *I tell you that in the same way there will be more rejoicing in heaven over one sinner who repents than over ninety-nine righteous persons who do not need to repent.*

Whether we accept it or not we are God's children, for He has created us. When we are away from God, it pains Him more than we can imagine for He does not want even a single one of His children to perish. In **John 6:38-39**, Jesus reveals God's will – *For I have come down from heaven not to do my will but to do the will of him who sent me. And this is the will of him who sent me, that I shall lose none of all that he has given me, but raise them up at the last day.*

God is longing for each one of His children to return to Him. He has prepared the way for us to be reconciled and He has prepared a celebration for our return because God delights in forgiving and restoring us.

Micah 7:18,

Who is a God like you,
who pardons sin and forgives the transgression
of the remnant of his inheritance?
You do not stay angry forever
but delight to show mercy.

5.   God's forgiveness is just

God's forgiveness is just and good because only God is holy and able to judge impartially. God knows everything. Nothing is hidden from Him. God is well acquainted with our ways and He is able to judge our motives. Only God can search our hearts and know our hidden thoughts.

Smita Valentina

We may question, how can a just God let the sinners go scot-free without any punishment? When we talk of the penalty of sin that Jesus Christ has taken upon himself once and for all, we must understand that it refers to the penalty of eternal death. **Romans 6:23** says – *For the wages of sin is death, but the gift of God is eternal life in Christ Jesus our Lord.*

Sin makes us unholy and separates us from God. Through Jesus Christ we are reconciled with God and saved from eternal separation. Everyone is going to experience physical death but for those who believe in Jesus Christ, we will be resurrected to eternal life.

However on earth we are not immune from the penalties we must face in accordance with the laws of the land. Bible says that all authority on earth is also set up by God. So, if a person commits murder, he will be tried for murder in accordance with the country's criminal law. If he seeks God's forgiveness with a sincere and repentant heart, God will forgive him and grant him eternal life; but on earth he will have to face the consequences of his sin.

Later, we will discuss the various elements of forgiveness. One of the elements is *Restoration*. God's justice requires that we make amends for our sins on earth. Further, God also disciplines us so that we do not err repeatedly. This is God's just forgiveness.

6. God's forgiveness is available to us by grace through faith in Jesus Christ

God's forgiveness is a gift of grace. No one who has received God's forgiveness can ever boast of his own merit or righteousness or anything else. **Ephesians 2:8-9** reiterates – *For it is by grace you have been saved, through faith – and this not from yourselves, it is the gift of God – not by works, so that no one can boast.*

And this grace, along with all the riches of the Kingdom of Heaven, is available to us only through Jesus Christ, as mentioned in **Ephesians 1:3-8** – *Praise be to the God and Father of our Lord Jesus Christ, who has blessed us in the heavenly realms with every spiritual blessing in Christ. For he chose us in him before the creation of the world to be holy and blameless in his sight. In love, he predestined us to be adopted as his sons through Jesus Christ, in accordance with his pleasure and will – to the praise of his glorious grace, which he has freely given us in the One he loves. In him we have redemption through his blood, the forgiveness of sins, in accordance with the riches of God's grace that he lavished on us with all wisdom and understanding.*

Shortly after Jesus Christ's ascension, Peter and John witnessed boldly before the Sanhedrin – *It is by the name of Jesus Christ of Nazareth, whom you crucified but whom God raised from the dead, that this man stands before you healed… Salvation is found in no one else, for there is no other name under heaven given to men by which we must be saved.* (Ref. **Acts 4:10-12**)

7.   God's forgiveness magnifies and glorifies him

Just as God's love is unfathomable, His forgiveness knows no bounds. When we approach God with a sincere, contrite heart, God's glorious grace in forgiveness enables us to realize how desperately we need Him in our lives.

True forgiveness is quite a rarity on earth but I am sure you would have experience something like this at least once in your life – *When I was in school I had a falling out with a very dear friend and senior. I was so angry with her that I vowed I won't speak to her ever again. One evening I had a very severe headache and I couldn't go to the study hall. A while later, my friend arrived with a pain balm and without a word, she just sat by my side and began massaging my head. Soon, we were crying. Apparently, she had looked around for me and someone had told her I had a headache. That moment I had realized what a wonderful friend she was to me.* I know that this incident has nothing to do with God's forgiveness but it just reminded me of how God's greatness became real to me when I accepted Jesus Christ as my personal Saviour and felt the burden of my sins roll away.

God's forgiveness enables us to become aware of the full extent of God's holiness, His immeasurable love, His sovereign will, His immense power and authority. The Psalmist sings of God's forgiveness in Psalm 130. Realising that despite God's ability to punish us, He chooses to offer full redemption to those who put their hope in Him; the Psalmist says in **Psalm 130:3-4** –

> *If you, O LORD, keep a record of sins,*
> *O Lord, who could stand?*
> *But with you there is forgiveness;*
> *therefore you are feared.*

Romans 5:20 highlights – *But where sin increased, grace increased all the more.* When we experience God's forgiveness, we can no longer continue in sin; instead, God's love in forgiving us inspires us to glorify Him through our holy lives.

HOW CAN WE RECEIVE GOD'S FORGIVENESS AND INHERIT ETERNAL LIFE?

God's forgiveness is His gracious gift and faithful promise to all who choose to accept His offer of salvation by believing in Jesus Christ. The most quoted verse on forgiveness and eternal life is **John 3:16** which says,

> *For God so loved the world that he gave his one and only Son, that whoever believes in him shall not perish but have eternal life.*

But what does *"believe in Jesus Christ"* encompass?

Jesus Christ's first message as he began his earthly ministry was: *The kingdom of God is near. Repent and believe the good news.* **(Mark 1:15)**

In **Matthew 19:16**, a rich young man asked Jesus, *"Teacher, what good thing must I do to get eternal life?"*

In **Matthew 19:21-26**, we find Jesus' final answer – *If you want to be perfect, go, sell your possessions and give to the poor, and you will have treasures in heaven. Then come, follow me... With man this is impossible, but with God all things are possible.*

What does *"following Jesus"* require?

The teachings of Jesus Christ are rooted in the greatest commandment – *Love the Lord your God and love one another.* According to Jesus, love is manifested through obedience. **John 14:21** notes – *Whoever has my commands and obeys them, he is the one who loves me. He who loves me will be loved by my Father, and I too will love him and show myself to him.*

We receive God's forgiveness through faith (i.e. believing in Jesus Christ), sincere repentance (i.e. turning away from sin and turning towards God) and obedience (i.e. following Jesus).

Faith and repentance go hand in hand. One cannot truly repent unless they become aware of their sinfulness. Faith brings that awareness. When Peter saw the great catch of fish, he became aware of Jesus' divinity and holiness. At the same time, he also became aware of his own sinfulness (Ref. **Luke 5:1-11**). We may have been hearing about Jesus all our life. Some of us who were born in Christian households grew up hearing about Jesus. But when faith comes, we believe and we are moved to repentance. And yes, faith comes through Jesus (Ref. **Acts 3:16**). Repentance and obedience are the fruits of faith. If we truly believe, we will repent and be obedient to God.

What should we believe about Jesus Christ? And, what does faith imply?

Many people believe that Jesus Christ was a good man. Some believe that he was a prophet and a great moral teacher. To many, Jesus was just like Buddha or Confucius or Mohammad or many other influential figures. I am sometimes much pained to see that even many seasoned Christians do not understand the full gravity of believing in Jesus Christ. For, most certainly, when faith comes we are led to believe that Jesus Christ is our Lord and God. And when we truly believe, we can no longer continue in our life of sin.

Colossians 1:15-20 highlights:

He is the image of the invisible God, the firstborn over all creation. For by him all things were created: things in heaven and on earth, visible and invisible, whether thrones or powers or rulers or authorities; all things were created by him and for him. He is before all things, and in him all things hold together. And he is the head of the body, the church; he is the beginning and the firstborn from among the dead, so that in everything he might have supremacy. For God was pleased to have all his fullness dwell in him, and through him to reconcile to himself all things, whether things on earth or things in heaven, by making peace through his blood, shed on the cross.

Full and complete knowledge of God and Jesus Christ is contained in the Bible. I encourage you to meditate on the Bible regularly to grow in your understanding of the Word of God and your living relationship with God. *Here, I would like to present before you the substance of our faith in Jesus Christ. This is the gospel that has been preached since Jesus Christ commissioned his disciples to be his witnesses to the ends of the earth; and this is the gospel that the Holy Spirit testifies to us.*

The Apostles' Messages

The Apostles and early disciples of Jesus Christ, who received direct commission from him to be his witness to the ends of the earth, proclaimed forgiveness and salvation in the Name of Jesus Christ.

As recorded in the Book of Acts, Apostle Peter delivered the first message of Salvation on the day the Holy Spirit came upon all the disciples who were gathered together in one place in Jerusalem. (Ref. **Acts 2**).

Quoting from the Scriptures, Peter proclaimed that Jesus is the One the prophets spoke of. **The important truths about Jesus Christ in Peter's message of Salvation are:**

- *Men of Israel, listen to this: Jesus of Nazareth was a man accredited by God to you by miracles, wonders and signs, which God did among you through him, as you yourselves know. This man was handed over to you by God's set purpose and foreknowledge; and you, with the help of wicked men, put him to death by nailing him to the cross. But God raised him from the dead, freeing him from the agony of death, because it was impossible for death to keep its hold on him.* **(Acts 2:22-24)**
- *God has raised this Jesus to life, and we are witnesses of the fact. Exalted to the right hand of God, he has received from the Father the promised Holy Spirit and has poured out what you now see and hear...* **(Acts 2:32-33)**
- *Therefore let all Israel be assured of this: God has made this Jesus, whom you crucified, both Lord and Christ.* **(Acts 2:36)**
- [When the people heard this, they were cut to the heart and said to Peter and the other apostles, "Brothers, what shall we do?"] **(Acts 2:37)**

    Peter replied, "Repent and be baptized, every one of you, in the name of Jesus Christ for the forgiveness of your sins. And you will receive the gift of the Holy Spirit. The promise is for you and your children and for all who are far off – for all whom the Lord our God will call." **(Acts 2:38-39)**

Smita Valentina

Jesus Christ's teachings in the Gospels

The four Canonical Gospels (i.e. Matthew, Mark, Luke and John) contain Jesus Christ's biography. They include the details of Jesus' ministry on earth, his teachings, his parables, his testimony, his suffering, crucifixion, death, resurrection and ascension.

The major part of the Synoptic Gospels (i.e. Matthew, Mark and Luke) cover the teachings of Jesus Christ that focus on the heart of God's law – **Love the Lord your God and love one another.** Jesus Christ explains God's law by connecting them all to the greatest commandment. He calls out the religious leaders and teachers for their show of religiosity – *You have let go of the commands of God and are holding on to the traditions of men.* **(Mark 7:8)**

Through his teachings, Jesus calls for **Obedience** – *So in everything, do to others what you would have them do to you, for this sums up the Law and the Prophets.* **(Matthew 7:12)**

Jesus also spoke through a lot of parables. Jesus' parables teach us about the Kingdom of God. They tell us about forgiveness, repentance, judgement, faith, fruitfulness and much more. Through the parables, Jesus reveals to us the desire of the Father to be reconciled to us. They reveal that we can repent and return to God through faith. Our faith and our repentance are expressed through obedience and fruitfulness which can be attained only when we are in a living relationship with God.

Jesus revealed his divinity and authority over the whole of creation through many signs and wonders that he performed during his ministry on earth. He healed the sick and raised the dead showing his power over sickness and death. He cast out evil spirits. He calmed the storm, walked on the waters and led Peter and his friends to the largest catch of fish they had ever seen. His miraculous signs prove the validity of Jesus' claim that he is the Son of God – *Do not believe me unless I do what my Father does. But if I do it, even though you do not believe me, believe the miracles, that you may know and understand that the Father is in me, and I in the Father.* **(John 10:37-38)**

All the four canonical gospels conclude with the crucifixion of Jesus on the Cross followed by his death, resurrection and ascension; thus, fulfilling the prophesies contained in the Old Testament. All point to Jesus Christ as the Promised Saviour.

The Gospel of John

The Gospel of John is highly schematic, as compared to the three synoptic gospels. In a meticulously planned manner, Apostle John provides deep insights into the life and teachings of Jesus Christ in the Gospel of John that contain direct references to Jesus as the Son of God. Out of the many miraculous signs that Jesus performed, John picks "Seven Signs" that show Jesus Christ's authority and power. The Gospel of John also contains the seven 'I AM' statements and discourses of Jesus Christ. These statements are his direct claims that He is the Son of God. John cites the purpose of his Gospel in **John 20:31** – *But these are written that you may believe that Jesus is the Christ, the Son of God, and that by believing you may have life in his name.*

These "Seven Signs" and Seven "I AM" statements summarize what we are called to believe. They are the full representation of Jesus Christ as our Saviour, Lord and God.

The Seven Signs and their spiritual significance

1.   **Jesus changes Water to Wine (John 2:1-11)**

At a wedding in Cana in Galilee, Jesus performed his first miraculous sign and revealed his glory. Seeing this, Jesus' disciples put their faith in him. The first sign demonstrates Jesus' power to make something new, to transform one substance to another. **Only Jesus, through whom all things were created, has the power to transform us into a new creation.**

2. Jesus heals the Official's Son (John 4:46-54)

Again at Cana, Jesus met a royal official whose son lay sick at Capernaum. The royal official begged Jesus to come and heal his son who was close to death. Jesus merely spoke the words and the official's son was healed at that instant. When the official realized this, he and all of his household believed. Jesus' second miraculous sign reveals that his word is enough. Just like the account of creation where God spoke and things came into being; Jesus demonstrated the same power by healing the official's son just by uttering: *'Your son will live'*. **Jesus has power over sickness and death and he is the source of all life on earth.**

3. The healing at Bethsaida (John 5:1-15)

Jesus healed a man who had been an invalid for thirty-eight years at Bethsaida in Jerusalem. This third miraculous sign reveals that no matter how terrible our condition is and how long we have been living in our terrible state, Jesus has the power to restore us. **No matter how sinful a person is; Jesus is able to make him spiritually alive and prepared for good works.** The only question we must answer is: *Do you want to get well?*

4. Jesus feeds the Five thousand (John 6:1-14)

The Jewish Passover Feast was near, and a great crowd of people followed Jesus because of the miraculous signs he had performed on the sick. There, by the shore of the Sea of Galilee, Jesus took five small barley loaves and two small fish (a small boy's meal) and multiplied it to feed over five thousand people. The people ate as much as they wanted and the disciples gathered and filled twelve baskets with leftovers. After the people saw this miraculous sign, they began to say – *Surely, this is the Prophet who is to come into the world.* This miraculous sign shows that **Jesus is our Provider and he is the One who sustains all spiritual life. He is infinite.**

5.   Jesus walks on the Water (John 6:15-21)

When the disciples were sailing across the lake towards Capernaum, the waters grew stormy. Then they saw Jesus approach the boat walking on the water. As Jesus got on the boat, immediately it reached the shore where they were heading. This miraculous sign proves Jesus' authority over nature. **Jesus is the Lord over all creation. Through Jesus we can overcome all the storms of life. Nothing can separate us from the love of God that is in Christ Jesus our Lord.**

6.   Jesus heals a man born blind (John 9:1-41)

Jesus and his disciples saw a man blind form birth and Jesus healed him saying - ... *this happened so that the work of God might be displayed in his life.* Along with this miraculous healing, Jesus proclaimed – *While I am in the world, I am the light of the world.* The healing of this blind man caused resentment amongst the legalistic Pharisees who accused Jesus of being a sinner and breaking the law. Therefore, Jesus spoke of spiritual blindness. Jesus had just performed a healing miracle – a clear sign of God's work – but the Pharisees were fixated on Jesus breaking the Sabbath by taking a small amount of mud to heal the blind man. This miraculous sign and the events surrounding it shows that **Jesus is the light of the world and just as he has the authority to give sight to the blind; he also has the authority and power to take away the sight of those who refuse to see.**

7.   Jesus raises Lazarus from the dead (John 11:1-57)

Lazarus was dead and he had been in the tomb for four days but Jesus called "Lazarus, come out!" and Lazarus came out of the grave, alive. Before performing this miraculous sign, Jesus looked up and said, *"Father, I thank you that you have heard me. I knew that you always hear me, but I said this for the benefit of the people standing here, that they may believe that you sent me."* Many who had come to visit Mary and Martha saw this miraculous sign and put their faith in Jesus. It proves that **Jesus is the giver of eternal life. Physical death is not the end for those who believe in Jesus Christ.**

These Seven Signs prove Jesus' lordship over all creation and over life, death and even eternal life. While these miracles are a clear sign of Jesus' power and authority proving that he is God, we can still refuse to believe and reject God's forgiveness and gift of salvation by hardening our hearts. Let us pray that God will help our unbelief and enable us to accept Jesus as our Saviour, Lord and God.

The Seven "I AM" Statements of Jesus Christ

These "I AM" statements resonate with God's revelation of Himself in the **Book of Exodus 3:14**. The most revered name of God in Hebrew – *Yahweh* – is the transliteration of 'I AM'.

[13]Moses said to God, "Suppose I go to the Israelites and say to them, 'The God of your fathers has sent me to you,' and they ask me, 'What is his name?' Then what shall I tell them?"

[14]God said to Moses, "I AM WHO I AM. This is what you are to say to the Israelites: 'I AM has sent me to you.'"

Jesus' "I AM" statements are his direct claim that He is God. They reveal his divinity and his mission. They also reveal Jesus Christ as the only One who can fulfil our spiritual needs and lead us to eternal life.

1.   I AM the bread of life – John 6:35, 41, 48, 51

[35]Then Jesus declared, "I am the bread of life. He who comes to me will never go hungry, and he who believes in me will never be thirsty.

[48]I am the bread of life.

[51]I am the living bread that came down from heaven. If anyone eats of this bread, he will live forever. This bread is my flesh, which I will give for the life of the world.

Jesus Christ gave his body as the atoning sacrifice for the sins of the world. Whoever believes that Jesus Christ died for him and accepts Jesus as his personal Saviour receives eternal life in Jesus Christ.

2.   I AM the light of the world – John 8:12

[12]When Jesus spoke again to the people, he said, "I am the light of the world. Whoever follows me will never walk in darkness, but will have the light of life."

Jesus Christ brings enlightenment. He reveals the truth about God and he reveals the darkness and evil that surrounds us. Jesus Christ gives our life the right direction and prevents us from getting lost in sin.

3.   I AM the gate for the sheep – John 10:7,9

[7]Therefore Jesus said again, "I tell you the truth, I am the gate for the sheep."

[9]"I am the gate; whoever enters through me will be saved. He will come in and go out, and find pasture."

Jesus is the only entry-point into the Kingdom of heaven. Only through Jesus can we enter and experience the full delights of salvation. It is also through Jesus Christ alone that we can identify with the members of God's church on earth and associate with the world more meaningfully and fruitfully.

4.   I AM the good shepherd – John 10:11, 14

[11]"I am the good shepherd. The good shepherd lays down his life for the sheep."

[14]"I am the good shepherd; I know my sheep and my sheep know me..."

Jesus is the only approved shepherd to lead us to eternal life. Therefore, those who believe in him must follow him obediently. Only by listening to Jesus' voice can we find sustenance for our souls and avoid falling out.

5.   I AM the resurrection and the life – John 11:25,26

[25]Jesus said to her, "I am the resurrection and the life. He who believes in me will live, even though he dies; [26]and whoever lives and believes in me will never die..."

Jesus points out the reality of resurrection and offers the promise of eternal life to those who believe in him. Only through Jesus we have the eternal hope of a resurrected life.

6.   I AM the way, the truth, and the life – John 14:6

Jesus answered, "I am the way and the truth and the life. No one comes to the Father except through me."

Jesus reveals the fullness of God. When we know Jesus personally, we become known to the Father. Nothing is hidden from us. Everything is revealed in the Bible. By faith, we accept that Jesus is God and find our way in him to eternal life.

7.   I AM the true vine – John 15:1,5

[1]"I am the true vine, and my Father is the gardener."

[5]"I am the vine; you are the branches. If a man remains in me and I in him, he will bear much fruit; apart from me you can do nothing."

Jesus invites us into a living and fruitful relation with him. Our deal with Jesus is not transactional. We cannot believe only for a little while and expect to receive a ticket to eternal life. Jesus reveals that we need his grace for our continued sustenance. Only by having a living and continued relationship with Jesus can we bear abundant fruit in keeping with true repentance. Jesus has promised to sustain us and make us fruitful if we remain in him.

This is the substance of our faith in Jesus Christ. A born-again Christian must believe that Jesus Christ is the full representation of God and he is our Lord and Saviour. Jesus took upon himself the sins of the whole world and paid the full price to redeem us from the slavery of sin. Now, we are bound to Jesus as our master for we were bought by him at a price – the hefty price of his own precious blood. Therefore, we are to obey Jesus faithfully.

Out of His great love and mercy, God has called us to be His children. Therefore, our obedience should not just stem out of servile fear but out of our reciprocal love for God. One who believes this, loves God and is obedient to God showing that he has received the fullness of God's forgiveness and become a new creation in Jesus Christ.

Smita Valentina

DIMENSIONS OF FORGIVENESS

God is the giver of all forgiveness and He has accomplished His part of the deal once and for all. But, for us forgiveness is a process. Even after being born-again in Christ Jesus, we will continue to sin because of ignorance or our spiritual weaknesses and immaturity. Therefore, on our part, forgiveness is an ongoing exercise.

Forgiveness requires:

A. **Reflection** – We need to reflect upon our lives on a day-to-day basis. It enables us to examine our thoughts, words, actions, inactions, relationships, meaningless activities, etc. It is through reflection that we realize our follies and lack of spiritual growth. Reflection also enables us to see where we are moving forward and brings encouragement. When we reflect upon our lives in the light of God's Word, we become aware of our spiritual condition.

   Lamentations 3:40 – *Let us examine our ways and test them, and let us return to the LORD.*

B. **Repentance** – Repentance means turning away from our sinful ways and turning towards God. Repentance consists of:

   a. **Conviction** – It is the Holy Spirit that convicts us of our sin. Conviction is being aware of the wrongs that we have done. For repentance to take place, conviction must lead to remorse.

   b. **Contrition** – Repentance requires a contrite heart. We must feel sorry for our wrongful actions. This remorse should not be self-directed i.e. we should not feel regretful because we will be punished if caught or because it will bring us shame. Rather, we must feel remorse that we have hurt or harmed others. Contrition comes from compassion.

c. **Confession** – Our conviction and contrition must lead to a confession of our sins. We must confess before God because all sin is directed towards God. We must also confess to the ones whom we have wronged. We must acknowledge our sin and seek their forgiveness.

d. **Correction** – Our repentance is half-hearted and incomplete if we do not attempt to reform our ways. Correction implies that we modify our behaviour so that we do not repeat our mistakes and sins again. God's discipline is the corrective process where God lets us face the consequences of our sins.

C. **Restoration** – Forgiveness is restorative. God offers forgiveness to us so that we can have a living relationship with Him. When we want to have restored relationship with God and with those whom we have wronged, we must make amends. Take an example: *Suppose you cheated a neighbour of their life-savings; a mere 'sorry' isn't going to restore your relationship with your neighbour. You must pay back the money you owe your neighbour.* In the Old Testament, God required offenders to pay an extra 20% to make amends. Zacchaeus, the tax collector in **Luke 19:1-10**, made restitution by giving half of his possessions to the poor, and promising to pay back four-times the amount to the people he had cheated.

Describing the righteousness that comes through faith, **Romans 10:9-10** notes: *That if you confess with your mouth, "Jesus is Lord," and believe in your heart that God raised him from the dead, you will be saved. For it is with your heart that you believe and are justified, and it is with your mouth that you confess and are saved.*

Smita Valentina

Believing isn't about just the knowledge of facts. It is a deeper conviction and trust in Jesus Christ as our only way to eternal life. Our true confession and sincere belief is reflected in our transformed life. Do not be fooled for God cannot be mocked or cheated. He searches our hearts.

Repent from your past misdeeds. Turn away from your life of sin and turn to Jesus in whom we have the guarantee of forgiveness and everlasting life. And, God will give you the Holy Spirit, your Counsellor, to teach you and remind you of all things and to complete the good work of sanctification in your life, so that you are transformed into the likeness of Jesus Christ with ever-increasing glory.

WHAT GOD'S FORGIVENESS DOES TO US?

All sin is directed towards God and forgiveness establishes peace with God. It is essentially an imagery of war. Sin is rebellion against God. When we come before God in repentance, it is a sign of our surrender to God. We lay down our arms and weapons before God – all our wickedness and evil ways – and resolve not to rebel again. And God makes a treaty of peace with us. This treaty of peace with God spells out the terms and conditions of our new formed relationship with God. We are no longer God's enemies. The unique terms of this peace treaty with God can be found in the Bible. Here, I have listed a few wonderful changes that occur when we receive God's forgiveness:

i.   **It restores our broken relationship with God**

The most wonderful thing that happens to us when we accept God's forgiveness is we are reconciled with God and we enter into a renewed living relationship with God. **Romans 5:10-11** – *For if, when we were God's enemies, we were reconciled to him through the death of his Son, how much more, having been reconciled, shall we be saved through his life! Not only*

Forgiveness

is this so, but we also rejoice in God through our Lord Jesus Christ, through whom we have now received reconciliation.

ii.   It imputes Jesus Christ's righteousness upon us

Now God no longer considers us as sinners but Jesus' righteousness is imputed on us which makes us blameless before God. **Romans 3:21-22** – *But now a righteousness from God, apart from law, has been made known, to which the Law and the Prophets testify. This righteousness from God comes through faith in Jesus Christ to all who believe.*

iii.   It grants us citizenship into God's Kingdom

Just like a victorious king takes over the subjects of the defeated kingdom; by surrendering to Jesus Christ, we become the subjects of God's Kingdom. We gain the full rights and privileges of citizenship in the Kingdom of Heaven. **Philippians 3:20-21** – *But our citizenship is in heaven. And we eagerly await a Saviour from there, the Lord Jesus Christ, who by the power that enables him to bring everything under his control, will transform our lowly bodies so that they will be like his glorious body.*

iv.   It makes us God's adopted children

Normally, the subjects of a defeated kingdom are inducted as slaves by the victorious King. Often we read that we are bought at a price. Usually, slaves are bought and sold. And while, we do not deserve anything more than the position of a slave in God's kingdom (as the prodigal son acknowledged); the Bible uses another term 'ransom' suggesting that God considers us more than slaves. Jesus says in **Matthew 20:28** - ... *the Son of Man did not come to be served, but to serve, and to give his life as a ransom for many.* We can only willingly pay a ransom for something or someone we love and value a lot. **Ephesians 1:4-5** – ... *In love he predestined us to be adopted as his sons through Jesus Christ, in accordance with his pleasure and will...*

Smita Valentina

v.   It makes us co-heirs with Jesus Christ

People adopt for various reasons. Sometimes people adopt orphans out of sympathy. They may provide for their needs and give them a good education so that they can build good careers. In very rare occasions an adopted child is treated equal to one's biological child. Though we are adopted as God's sons, God does not withhold anything from us. We are not just sons or mere heirs inheriting a small fraction of the father's wealth; Bible tells us we are co-heirs with Jesus Christ, the firstborn. **Romans 8:17** – *Now if we are children, then we are heirs – heirs of God and co-heirs with Christ, if indeed we share in his sufferings in order that we may also share in his glory.*

God's forgiveness grants us many privileges and rights as mentioned above. At the same time, it also lays upon us certain duties and responsibilities. To receive the above mentioned privileges we have to let go of our old ways and conform to the requirements of the citizenship of God's Kingdom.

vi.   We come under God's protection

Often, when a nation defeats another nation in a war, the defeated nation is asked to demilitarize. When we receive God's forgiveness and become God's children, we forego the right to get even with those who hurt us. Now God is our avenger. We ought to let God deal with those who hurt us. Jesus commands us not to judge anyone **(Matthew 7:1)**. Instead, we are called to show mercy, for mercy triumphs over judgement **(James 2:13)**. Further, **James 4:12** emphasises – *There is only one Lawgiver and Judge, the one who is able to save and destroy.*

vii. We no longer conform to the patterns of this world

Jesus' famous *"Beatitudes"* is a glimpse of the wide gap between the value system of this world and that of God's Kingdom. The laws of God's Kingdom are very different from the ways of this world. As we transition to God's Kingdom we need to be transformed to fit into God's value system. **Romans 12:2** says – *Do not conform any longer to the pattern of this world, but be transformed by the renewing of your mind. Then you will be able to test and approve what God's will is – his good, pleasing and perfect will.*

viii. We must say no to all ungodliness and lay aside all that binds

God is holy and no ungodliness can exist in God's presence. By accepting God's forgiveness, we make a choice to be in God's presence and away from all ungodliness. God knows our weakness and therefore, He has given us the Holy Spirit which empowers us to live godly live. We must consciously choose to exercise the power of the Holy Spirit in our lives each day. **Titus 2:11-12** says – *For the grace of God that brings salvation has appeared to all men. It teaches us to say "No" to ungodliness and worldly passions, and to live self-controlled, upright and godly lives in this present age.*

Hebrew 12:1 reiterates – *Therefore, since we are surrounded by such a great cloud of witnesses, let us throw off everything that hinders and the sin that so easily entangles, and let us run with perseverance the race marked out for us.*

ix. We serve God and God's church on earth

Though we have the citizenship of the Kingdom of God, we are still in the world as long as we are alive in our earthly bodies. But, we owe our full and unwavering allegiance to God. Even while on earth, our priority is to honour God and obey Him. Our goal is to please God rather than people. Therefore, even though threatened and persecuted, the

Apostles claimed – *Judge for yourselves whether it is right in God's sight to obey you rather than God* **(Acts 4:19)** and *We must obey God rather than men* **(Acts 5:29).**

Later, **Colossians 3:23-24** notes – *Whatever you do, work at it with all your heart, as working for the Lord, not for men, since you know that you will receive an inheritance from the Lord as a reward. It is the Lord Christ you are serving.*

x.   We become God's ambassadors on earth

As born-again Christians, who have accepted God's forgiveness and salvation, we are not ordinary people on this earth. God has placed us here on earth in various positions as His ambassadors. Therefore, we are God's representatives who are tasked to carry God's message of peace and reconciliation through Jesus Christ. Our lives on earth must reflect the standards of the Kingdom of Heaven and glorify our Heavenly Father, our eternal King.

2 Corinthians 5:17-20 – *Therefore, if anyone is in Christ, he is a new creation; the old has gone, the new has come! All this is from God, who reconciled us to himself through Christ and gave us the ministry of reconciliation: that God was reconciling the world to himself in Christ, not counting men's sins against them. And he has committed to us the message of reconciliation. We are therefore Christ's ambassadors, as though God were making his appeal through us. We implore you on Christ's behalf: Be reconciled to God.*

A FORGIVING HEART

God's perfect forgiveness and salvation turns our heart of stone to a compassionate and forgiving heart. This transformation is not instantaneous. It is a slow and painful process. Imagine trying to fit into a new prosthetic limb. In the beginning, it is so difficult that we will continually try to remove the prosthetic limb, even against doctor's advice. But with time, our wound heals and the pain reduces considerably. I have talked to a few people with prosthetics and they say that after a while the prosthetics seem like an extension of their own bodies. Sometimes the prosthetic limb may still give you some discomfort but by then, you are well aware that you no longer want to discard it.

A forgiving heart is a sign that we have accepted full forgiveness from God and we have surrendered our all to God. If we are struggling to forgive others, we need to introspect and focus on these vital truths that are essential to our spiritual maturity:

a. **Forgiving those who have hurt us is not optional for God's children**

The assurance of our forgiveness from God depends on whether we imitate God in forgiving others or not. Jesus taught his disciples how to pray. This prayer is popularly known as **"The Lord's Prayer"** and every Christian has committed it to memory. In the Lord's Prayer, **Matthew 6:12** says, *"Forgive us our debts, as we forgive our debtors."* Jesus expounds it in **Matthew 6:14-15** - *For if you forgive men when they sin against you, your heavenly Father will also forgive you. But if you do not forgive men their sins, your Father will not forgive your sins.*

You can understand this like the terms and conditions of a guarantee or a warranty. We can enjoy the benefits of the *guarantee* or *warranty* if we agree to the terms and conditions and obey them. God has already extended that guarantee of eternal life. It is up to us to retain the privileges of God's offer or forfeit them.

"Forgiving others" is an essential condition for the full realization of God's promises in our lives.

Smita Valentina

b. Our ability to forgive others is a sign of our spiritual growth

Forgiveness is an expression of sacrificial love. There's a famous adage: *To err is human, to forgive divine.* Truly, the love that's required to forgive those who have hurt us comes from God alone. When we begin sharing God's love and forgiveness with others, it's a sure sign that we are becoming more and more like Jesus Christ.

c. Christians are called to demonstrate Christ-like forgiveness

We are called to be imitators of Jesus Christ. But, there are two aspects of our life where we are specifically called to demonstrate Christ-likeness: Love and Forgiveness.

Jesus says in **John 13:34** – *A new command I give you: Love one another. As I have loved you, so you must love one another.*

Ephesians 4:32 says – *Be kind and compassionate to one another, forgiving each other, just as in Christ God forgave you.* (also ref. **Colossians 3:12-13**)

We are called to forgive just as we have been forgiven by God. Our own kind of forgiveness may be very different from God's forgiveness. Sometimes, we just say a very superficial 'sorry' and feel we have forgiven others. That is not the kind of forgiveness God commands us to extend to others. Our forgiveness must be genuine and complete just as God's forgiveness towards us.

d. Therefore, to be able to forgive others, we must remember how much we have been forgiven

Luke 7:36-50 tells us of the woman who washed Jesus' feet with her tears and poured expensive perfume on them. Commending her love and faith, Jesus says in **Luke 7:47** – *Therefore, I tell you, her many sins have been forgiven – for she* *loved much. But he who has been forgiven little loves little.* How much more should we love for we have been forgiven so fully and so perfectly! And how much more obedient should we be to God when we love much!

Colossians 3:12-13 exhorts us to bear with each other – *Therefore, as God's chosen people, holy and dearly loved, clothe yourselves with compassion, kindness, humility, gentleness and patience. Bear with each other and forgive whatever grievances you may have against one another. Forgive as the Lord forgave you.*

Remember God's infinite patience with us that is still continuing in our lives. We aren't perfect yet, but God continues to show us His sustained love and compassion. What were we that the Son of God should come down on earth and bear our sins upon himself? But, Jesus demonstrated exemplary humility on earth and on the Cross. A continual reminder of God's abundant grace should spur us to inculcate a forgiving heart.

The consequences of an unforgiving heart

Nothing sums up our cardinal requirement to forgive, and the repercussions of being unmerciful, better than the *Parable of the Unmerciful Servant* – **Matthew 18:21-35**

A king forgave one of his servants who owed him ten thousand talents, since he was unable to pay. When the servant begged for mercy, the king took pity on him and cancelled his debt. However, this same servant found one of his fellow servants who owed him a hundred *denarii* and he demanded his money back. When the fellow servant was unable to pay, the unmerciful servant refused to show any pity and had his fellow servant thrown into prison.

Jesus concludes the parable in **Matthew 18:32-35** – *Then the master called the servant in. "You wicked servant," he said, "I cancelled all that debt of yours because you begged me to.*

Smita Valentina

Shouldn't you have had mercy on your fellow servant just as I had on you?" In anger his master turned him over to the jailers to be tortured, until he should pay back all he owed. "This is how my heavenly Father will treat each of you unless you forgive your brother from your heart."

There are two aspects of forgiveness that people are often confused about. Let us take a quick look into these two aspects:

How many times should we forgive someone?

Matthew 18:21-22 highlights a Q&A between Peter and Jesus:

Then Peter came to Jesus and asked, "Lord, how many times shall I forgive my brother when he sins against me? Up to seven times?"

Jesus answered, "I tell you, not seven times, but seventy-seven times."

Luke 17:3-4 also makes a note of it:

"If your brother sins, rebuke him, and if he repents, forgive him. If he sins against you seven times in a day, and seven times comes back to you and says, 'I repent', forgive him."

Jesus wants to make it clear that *'the number of times'* does not matter. We must forgive repeatedly without keeping a count. Just as God's forgiveness is always available to us; our forgiveness should always be available to others. By offering our forgiveness, we experience perfect peace in Christ Jesus.

In our heart we must forgive others even though they do not demonstrate any remorse because we do not have the right to withhold our forgiveness from anyone. Remember, God is the only Lawgiver and Judge. However, Luke's rendition of *'how many times we must forgive others'* gives us a better perspective into how this forgiveness is expressed outwardly:

I. The first point that Jesus makes is: **Rebuke**. If we see someone sinning, whether against us or against anyone else, we must rebuke them. This admonition is corrective and constructive. It is not to shame our offenders but to gently guide them towards truth and Christ's righteousness. Our rebuke should not create a chasm between us and our offenders; rather it should restore peace and goodwill.

II. The second criteria for the extension of this repeated forgiveness is *'repentance'*. Our offender must show remorse. No matter how gently we admonish our offenders and no matter how reasonable we are; there's no guarantee that our offenders will accept our correction. Often, we will come across people who will never admit that they are wrong. When there's no awareness of guilt, there's no scope for forgiveness.

III. The third criteria is *'return'*. If our offender returns to us seeking our forgiveness; we must forgive. Our offender may have ignored our admonition or even abused us for our correction; but if they realize their mistake and return, we must forgive.

Note: *When an offense concerns us, the criterion of 'rebuke' stands valid through and through. However, if an offense doesn't concern us, it is prudent to use discretion and discernment. We may not be aware of the circumstances surrounding the offense and instead of being a peacemaker; we may end up being a rioter.*

Should we let others hurt us repeatedly?

This second aspect of forgiveness stems from the first one. Often, many Christians do not understand Jesus' teaching of forgiving our offenders without keeping a count and end up getting hurt repeatedly. I am not talking about just emotional hurts. Many Christians continue to live in toxic relationships enduring physical abuse. We may have such toxic relationships with our abusive spouses or siblings or friends and relatives, and sometimes, even parents. Above, we saw a few criteria that are essential for a fruitful forgiving experience.

Jesus tells us about another set of criteria where we are freed from the burden of continuing in toxic relationships. In **Matthew 18:15-17**, Jesus tells us how to deal with someone who refuses to listen and repent:

"If your brother sins against you, go and show him his fault, just between the two of you. If he listens to you, you have won your brother over. But if he will not listen, take one or two others along, so that 'every matter may be established by the testimony of two or three witnesses.' If he refuses to listen even to the church, treat him as you would a pagan or a tax collector."

Though we are expected to demonstrate Christ-likeness in all aspects of our life, it is alright to admit that we are not Christ. We are human and we have limitations. It is alright to walk out of a toxic relationship if your efforts and willingness to forgive is not reciprocated by repentance and transformation of your offender. It is alright to distance yourself from your offender if it puts you in danger. God has not decreed that you suffer at the hands of an abuser because you have chosen to love and forgive.

Understanding the corruption and dangers of the world, Jesus also warns his disciples in **Matthew 10:16** – *I am sending you out like sheep among wolves. Therefore be as shrewd as snakes and as innocent as doves.*

There will be people who will feign repentance to take advantage of you. There will be people who will cheat you because your graceful disposition and compassion is considered weakness in the world. Therefore, we need to exercise caution. Jesus tells us to be shrewd and not fall prey to the craftiness of wicked people.

One of the greatest degeneration of our times is, what I call, *'cushioning of sin'*. New labels are emerging regularly that classify sinful ways as diseases or alternative lifestyles. They have socio-political backing and they have a significant impact on economy. The most adverse fallout of this *'cushioning of sin'* is we are asked to sympathise with and accommodate those who indulge in such sinful ways. I am sure most of you would have come across people who are addicted to alcohol or drugs or casual sex. If they continue to ignore your counsel, the Word of God tells you to *'shake the dust off your feet when you leave'* for their judgement will be on their own heads **(Matthew 10:14).**

FRUITFULNESS THROUGH FORGIVENESS

John the Baptist preached: *"Repent, for the kingdom of heaven is near." "Produce fruit in keeping with repentance." "The axe is already at the root of the trees, and every tree that does not produce good fruit will be cut down and thrown into the fire."* **(Matthew 3:2,8,10)**

Spiritual fruitfulness is a sign and proof of sincere repentance and our full acceptance of the gift of forgiveness.

I propagate a lot of *Pothos* cuttings and I am quite generous in gifting my propagated plants to those who show admiration for them. There are some who take care of the plants and soon they begin propagating their own cuttings. However, there are some who are quite negligent. They forget to water their plants. Often, they would leave the plant in scorching sunlight. Even if they manage to keep their plant alive, they struggle a lot. Then there are some who are averse

Smita Valentina

to pruning and propagating. They would rather let their plant grow leggy or sprawl wildly than share cuttings with others.

Sometimes, when I tend my small balcony garden, I ponder over forgiveness. My *Golden Pothos* comes from a very old mother plant from my village. I received it freely and though there has been a lot of challenge in keeping it alive and thriving because of our frequent transfers; it's very precious to me. It's a reminder of home; and now, a metaphor for 'forgiveness'. The forgiveness that we have received from God must be valued because even though it did not cost us a penny, Jesus paid for it with his blood on the Cross. We must ensure to follow the directions to keep this forgiveness alive and meaningful in our lives at all cost. We must let it produce an abundance of spiritual fruit in our life. Just as we received God's forgiveness freely, we must also grow in our willingness to forgive freely. At the end, we will be counted faithful if have managed to keep God's forgiveness alive in our life.

Jesus tells us in **John 15:4-6** – *Remain in me, and I will remain in you. No branch can bear fruit by itself; it must remain in the vine. Neither can you bear fruit unless you remain in me. I am the vine; you are the branches. If a man remains in me and I in him, he will bear much fruit; apart from me you can do nothing. If anyone does not remain in me, he is like a branch that is thrown away and withers; such branches are picked up, thrown into the fire and burned.*

God's forgiveness grafts us into the vine i.e. Jesus Christ. It is the beginning of our journey towards fruitfulness that God expects of us. When a branch is connected to a vine, it draws its nourishment from the vine. When we are grafted into Jesus Christ, his commands and teachings through the guidance and power of the Holy Spirit provide us with the nourishment to grow and be fruitful. If we reject the nourishment that Jesus provides us, we will wither away.

Further, a tree doesn't produce all its fruits for its own benefit. It produces an abundance of fruits for others. Our spiritual fruitfulness must be a blessing for others around us.

Galatians 5:22-23 cites the nine qualities of the spiritual fruit – **love, joy, peace, patience, kindness, goodness, faithfulness, gentleness and self-control**.

2 Peter 1:5-9 also cites some of these qualities and says – *For if you possess these qualities in increasing measure, they will help you from being ineffective and unproductive in your knowledge of our Lord Jesus Christ. But if anyone does not have them, he is nearsighted and blind, and has forgotten that he has been cleansed from his past sins.*

Let us, therefore, always remember God's great love in offering forgiveness to us and continue to hold on to the great promise and hope of salvation we have as we remain firmly rooted in Jesus Christ. Let us continue to spur one another to bear much fruit so that we will have full confidence before God and men and glorify God proving we are Jesus Christ's disciples.

John 15:7-8 – *If you remain in me and my words remain in you, ask whatever you wish, and it will be given you. This is to my Father's glory, that you bear much fruit, showing yourselves to be my disciples.*

****

Smita Valentina

Jesus touched me

Every day, every moment
Jesus asked me to look into His eyes.
He wanted to tell me something,
But I never dared to reply.

I was afraid He would expose my sins
I never wanted to display.
I was afraid He would ask for something
I never wanted to give away.

But when I looked into His loving eyes;
There were no accusations, no demands.
They said silently, "I love you";
And He enfolded me in His bleeding hands.

Poem 40 from *Bougainvilleas and Sparrows*

References

I use the following resources for my personal Bible study and meditations:

1. NIV Quest Study Bible, Revised, Copyright © 1994, 2003 by The Zondervan Corporation
2. The New Strong's Exhaustive Concordance of the Bible by James Strong, LL.D, S.T.D., Copyright © 1995, 1996 by Thomas Nelson Publishers
3. NKJV Cultural Backgrounds Study Bible Copyright © 2017 by Zondervan

Smita Valentina